LOOKING BACK

by
HUDSON TAYLOR

AN AUTOBIOGRAPHY

Formerly titled
A RETROSPECT

Edited for modern English
by
M. E. Tewksbury

© OMF INTERNATIONAL
(formerly China Inland Mission)
Published by Overseas Missionary Fellowship Inc.
10 W. Dry Creek Circle, Littleton, CO 80120

Published 2003

OMF Books are distributed by:
OMF, 10 West Dry Creek Circle, Littleton, CO 80120, USA
OMF, Station Approach, Borough Green, Sevenoaks, Kent TN15
8BG, UK
OMF, 5155 Spectrum Way, Bldg. 21, Mississauga, ON
L4W 5A1, Canada
OMF, PO Box 849, Epping, NSW 2121, Australia
OMF, PO Box 10159, Auckland, New Zealand
OMF, PO Box 3080, Pinegowrie 2123, South Africa
and other OMF offices
Website: www.omf.org

ISBN 1-929122-19-5

CREDITS:

FOREWORD

BY HUDSON TAYLOR

THE FOLLOWING STORY TELLS SOME of the experiences that eventually led to forming the China Inland Mission. These experiences also show why the Mission turned out the way it did. These stories first appeared in *China's Millions* [CIM's monthly magazine]. Many of the people who read them in the magazine asked if we could print the story separately. Miss Guinness incorporated it in a book that gave the story up to the beginning of 1894.

But since friends kept asking for it in the form of a pamphlet they could distribute widely, we brought out this edition.

We drew a lot of the material for this book from speeches given in China during a conference of our missionaries. This is why it is written in a direct narrative form. We didn't think we needed to change that.

"Remember how the Lord your God led you all the way..."
(Deuteronomy 8:2).

CHAPTER ONE

THE POWER OF PRAYER

WHEN WE DO CHRISTIAN WORK, what counts is to keep looking at God. God's work isn't so much about what man does for God. It's about what God does through man. We are privileged—God's co workers.

Preaching the good news and spreading truth are good for our sick world. Even so, we shouldn't forget the most important thing, which is obeying God and glorifying his name. And making our Father's heart happy by living and working as though we are well-loved children.

Many events in my early life brought this lesson home to me. Thinking over my own life reminds me how much missionary work owes to people who will never go to the mission field. Many of them can't give much. In fact, they're in for a surprise. On the great day when Jesus comes again, they'll see how much the work advanced because of their love, sympathy and prayers.

I owe a lot to my dear parents, who have passed

away—entered into rest. But the influence of their lives will never pass away.

A long time ago, probably around 1830, China's spiritual condition touched my father's heart. He was a dedicated and successful evangelist in England at the time. He read several books about China. One was on the travels of Captain Basil Hall.

My father's situation kept him from going to serve in China himself. But he prayed that if God gave him a son, God would call him to work in that huge needy empire.

I didn't know about my father's prayer until I returned to England more than seven years after I first sailed for China. This prayer had been prayed before I was born. How interesting to see the way God answered it.

For many years my parents gave up any thought of me becoming a missionary because of my poor health. But when the right time came God improved my health. In fact, I didn't die in China like some did. And God has given me strength for hard work, while many stronger men and women have gone under.

As a child, I had many opportunities to learn the value of prayer and of God's word. My parents liked to point out that if God existed, the smartest thing to do was to trust him, obey him and serve him with total dedication. But that still didn't change my heart.

I often tried to make myself into a Christian. Of course I failed. Finally I started to think I couldn't be saved, for some reason. The best I could do, I thought, was to get all I could from the world. There was no hope for me after the grave.

During that time I met some people who were skeptics—they didn't believe. I accepted what they taught, only too thankful to think I could escape the doom that waited for unbelievers—if my parents and the Bible were right.

It may seem strange to say this, but I've often felt thankful for the experience of being skeptical. Many Christians say they believe the Bible, but they're satisfied with living as though the Bible doesn't exist. The inconsistency in their lives was one of the strongest arguments used by my skeptical friends. At the time, I often felt—and said—that if I pretended to believe the Bible, I would at least try to live by it. I would put it to the test fairly. If it failed to prove true and reliable, I would throw it out completely.

I stuck with this idea when the Lord brought me to himself. I think I can say that since that time I have put God's word to the test. It has never failed me. I have never had any reason to regret believing its promises or following its guidance.

LET ME TELL YOU HOW GOD answered the prayers of my dear mother and sister for my conversion. I'll never forget that day.

I was about fifteen years old. Since my mother was away from home, I had a holiday. That afternoon I looked through my father's library for a book—to kill time. Nothing attracted me. I turned over a little basket of pamphlets, and picked out a gospel tract that looked interesting. "There'll be a story at the beginning," I told myself. "And a sermon or moral at the end. I'll read the story and leave the end for those who like that kind of stuff."

I sat down to read the little book without any worries. If salvation existed, I didn't think it was for me. I distinctly remember meaning to put the tract down as soon as it got preachy.

In those days, a lot of people called conversion, "getting serious." If you looked at the faces of some so-called Christians, it seemed very serious. Wouldn't it be great if God's people always had faces that clearly showed the happiness of salvation? Then unconverted people would call conversion "getting joyful" instead of "getting serious."

Little did I know, at the time, what was going on in my dear mother's heart. She was seventy or eighty miles away. She got up from the dinner table that afternoon with an intense desire for her boy to be converted. Since she was away from home and had more free time than usual, she felt she had a special opportunity to plead with God for me. She went to her room and turned the key in the door. She decided she would not leave that spot until God answered her prayers.

Hour after hour she pleaded for me. Finally she couldn't pray any longer. Instead, the Spirit moved her to praise God for what had already happened—her only son's conversion.

Meanwhile, as I mentioned, something had led me

to pick up this little tract. While reading it, the sentence, "The finished work of Christ" struck me.

A thought passed through my mind: Why does the writer use that expression? Why not say "the atoning or propitiatory work of Christ"?

Right away, the words, "It is finished" suggested themselves to my mind.

What was finished?

I answered immediately, "A complete and perfect atonement and satisfaction for sin. The Substitute paid the debt. Christ died for our sins. 'And not only for ours but also for the sins of the whole world.'" (1 John 2:2)

Then the thought came: If the whole work was finished and the whole debt paid, what's left for me to do?

Light flashed into my soul. The happy realization dawned. There was nothing in the world I could do except fall on my knees and accept this Savior and his salvation. And to praise him forever.

So while my dear mother was praising God on her knees in her room, I was praising him in the old warehouse where I had gone to read.

Several days passed. I told my sister about my happiness, but only after she promised not to tell anyone. When our dear mother came home two weeks later, I met her at the door. I wanted to tell her I had good news.

I can still almost feel her arms around my neck as she hugged me. "I know, my boy;" she said, "I've been rejoicing two weeks about the good news you have for me."

"Why?" I asked in surprise, "Did Amelia break her promise? She said she wouldn't tell anyone."

My mother assured me she hadn't learned the news from any human source. She went on to tell me what had happened while she prayed.

You have to agree. It would be strange if I didn't believe in the power of prayer.

But that wasn't all. A little while later, I picked up a journal just like one I had. I thought it was mine, so I opened it. Something caught my eye. It was a few lines from an entry in the little diary, which belonged to my sister. She'd written that she would pray every day for her brother's conversion until God answered. Exactly one month later, the Lord turned me from darkness to light.

With people like that around me, and because I was converted through prayer, maybe it was natural for me to feel that God's promises are very real. And that prayer is a matter-of-fact business deal with God. I felt like this from the beginning of my Christian life.

CHAPTER TWO

THE CALL TO SERVICE

AFTER A WHILE, THE FIRST JOY OF conversion passed. A painful soul deadness followed, and a lot of conflict.

This ended, too. It left me with a greater feeling of my own weakness and dependence on the Lord. He is the only one who saves his people and keeps them. When the soul struggles with sin, then gets tired and disappointed, the calm rest that comes from trusting in the Shepherd of Israel is so sweet.

Several months after my conversion I had a free afternoon. I closed myself in my room. I wanted to spend the afternoon mostly talking with God. Feeling pretty happy, I poured my soul out to God. Over and over, I told him about my love for him. I felt so thankful! He had done everything for me. He'd saved me when I had given up all hope. I hadn't even wanted salvation!

I asked him to give me something to do for him. I wanted an outlet for my love and thankfulness. I wanted some self-denying way to serve him. It didn't matter what it was. Or if it was difficult or unimportant. I wanted something that would please him. Something I could do for the One who had done so much for me.

I remember that I dedicated myself without holding anything back. I put myself, my life, my friends, everything on the altar. A deep, solemn sort of feeling came over me. With it came assurance. I knew God had accepted my offering. His presence became real and blessed. I was only a child—only fifteen—but I remember stretching myself on the ground and lying there, silent, before him. I felt indescribable awe and joy.

I didn't know what kind of service he accepted me for, but a deep sense of awareness came over me. I didn't belong to myself any more.

This feeling of not being my own has never left me. It's been very practical. Two or three years later, I received an unusually good offer to study medicine. The only condition was that I become a certain doctor's apprentice. He was, at that time, my friend and teacher. But I didn't dare accept the offer. It was a binding agreement and I wasn't my own to give away. I felt like I had to keep myself always free, at the disposal of the One I belonged to. I never knew when or how he might call me to service.

A few months after this dedication time, God impressed an idea into my soul. The Lord wanted me in China. The work would probably cost me my life.

In those days, China was not as open as it is now. Few missions had workers there. I couldn't get my hands on many books about missions in China either. I learned, however, that the Congregational minister of my home town owned a copy of Medhurst's *China*. I called on him to ask him to lend me the book. He agreed. "Why do you want to read it?" he asked.

"God has called me to spend my life as a missionary there," I told him.

"And how do you plan to go there?" he asked.

"I have no idea," I told him. Then I added that I would probably need to do what the twelve disciples, and the seventy, had done in Judea. I would go without a "purse or bag." I would have to rely on the One who had called me. He would supply everything I needed.

The minister put his hand on my shoulder. "Ah, my boy," he said kindly, "as you grow older you will get wiser than that. That idea would do okay in the days when Christ himself was on earth. But not now."

I have grown older since then, but not wiser. I am more convinced than ever that if we follow the directions our Master gave his first disciples, and believe the promises, we will find them just as appropriate now as they were then.

MEDHURST'S BOOK ON CHINA emphasized the value of medical missions in China. This made me think that studying medicine was a valuable way to get ready.

My dear parents didn't discourage or encourage my desire to do missionary work. They advised me to use everything I could to grow in body, mind, heart and soul. They also told me to wait on God, to be willing to let him show me I was wrong. They told me to follow his guidance, and to go forward only if and when he opened the way to be a missionary.

Since then, I have often proved the importance of this advice. I began to exercise more outdoors, to strengthen my body. I got rid of my featherbed and tried do without as many other home comforts as I could. I did all this to get myself ready for a rougher life. I also began to do whatever Christian work I could. I handed out tracts, taught Sunday school and visited the poor and sick.

After studying at home to prepare for it, I went to Hull for training in medicine and surgery. In Hull, I became the assistant to a doctor connected with the Hull School of Medicine. He was also the surgeon for several factories. This brought many accident cases to our dispensary, and gave me the opportunity to see and practice minor surgery.

I have to mention one event that also happened here. Before I left home, the subject of tithing caught my attention. This meant setting aside the first fruits of my wages, and also some of my belongings, for the Lord's service.

I thought it was a good idea to see what the Bible said about it before I left home. After I left home, I knew I might end up in a situation that could bias my decisions by pressuring me with needs and desires. The Lord led me to set aside at least one tenth of all I earned or received for serving him.

My salary as a medical assistant in Hull would have

let me do this easily. But the family situation of my kind friend and employer changed. I had to live somewhere else.

They found a comfortable place for me with a relative. Then they added the exact amount to my salary that I needed to pay for my room and board.

Now the question came to my mind: Should I tithe this amount also? It must be a part of my income. If it was government income tax, it would be included. On the other hand, to take a tithe from the whole amount wouldn't leave me enough for other things.

For a while I was embarrassed. I didn't know what to do. After a lot of thought and prayer God led me to leave the comfortable place and the agreeable people I lived with. I rented a little place in the suburbs, a living room and bedroom in one. Now I could tithe my whole income easily.

The change affected me quite a bit, but blessing came with it. Since I was alone, I had more time to study God's word. I could visit the poor more, and do more evangelistic work on summer evenings. I met many people in bad situations. I soon saw that it was a privilege to live on even less and give away much more than I had meant to give at first. I didn't find it hard at all.

ABOUT THIS TIME, A FRIEND RAISED the question of the coming of our Lord Jesus Christ, in person and before the millennium. He gave me a list of passages on the subject, without any notes or comments, and told me to think about it.

I spent a lot of time studying the scriptures about it. God showed me that the same Jesus who left our earth in his resurrection body will come again in the same way. His feet will stand on the Mount of Olives. He will take his ancestor David's earthly throne, a throne promised before his birth.

In addition, I noticed that all through the New Testament, the Lord's coming was his people's one big hope. It was always given as the strongest motive for dedication and service. It was the greatest comfort in trouble.

I also learned that the time of his return for his people has not been revealed. It is their privilege to live a life of waiting for the Lord, from day to day and hour to hour. So in a way, it wasn't important when he came. The important thing was to be ready for him, so that you could joyfully account for what you had done for him, no matter when he appeared.

This hope had a completely practical effect on me. It led me to look carefully through my little library to see if I had any books I didn't need any more. I also went through my small closet. I wanted to be absolutely sure that if the Master came right away, I wouldn't be sorry about anything I had. My library shrank considerably, to the benefit of some poor neighbors—and to my own soul's even greater benefit. I also discovered that I had clothes someone else would get more use out of.

Every now and then, whenever I can, I have found it helpful to repeat this sorting process. Every time I have gone from basement to attic, sorting out what I didn't need, I've received spiritual joy and blessing. I think we're all in danger of accumulating things we don't need that others could use. We may collect things without thinking or because of work pressures. But to keep them means we lose blessing.

If all the resources of God's church were used, how much more could get done! How many poor could we feed and clothe. How many of the unreached might hear the gospel. I recommend this sorting out. Do it in your mind all the time. And whenever possible, it's useful to do in a practical way too.

CHAPTER THREE

PREPARATION FOR SERVICE

BY NOW I HAD A DUAL PURPOSE IN mind. I would get used to enduring hard times and I would also save money. This would let me give even more help to the people I spent so much time sharing the gospel with.

I soon discovered I could live on a lot less than I had thought. I stopped using butter, milk and other similar luxuries. By living mainly on oatmeal and rice, and occasionally something else, I found that a little money was enough to meet my needs. That way I had more than two-thirds of my income free for other things.

The less I spent on myself, and the more I gave away, the more blessed and happy I felt. All day long, every day, I experienced indescribable joy. My God was a living, bright reality. All I had to do was serve. And I enjoyed it!

But it still seemed extremely serious to think about going to China. I would be far from every kind of human support. I would have to depend only on the living God, for protection, for supplies. For every other

kind of help, too. I felt if as my spiritual muscles needed strengthening for that to happen.

Of course, God wouldn't fail if faith didn't. But what
if my faith wasn't enough? I hadn't learned yet that
even "if we are faithless, he will remain faithful, for he
cannot disown himself" (2 Timothy 2:13). So though I
didn't question his faithfulness, I seriously questioned
whether my faith was strong enough to do what God
had called me to do.

"When I get out to China," I thought, "I won't be
able to call on anyone for any need. I'll only be able to
call on God. So before I leave England, it's really important for me to learn to move man, through God, by
prayer alone!"

My boss at Hull, a kind man, was always busy. He
wanted me to remind him when it came time for him to
pay my salary. I decided not to do it directly. Instead, I
would ask God to remind him. That way, the answered
prayer would encourage me.

One time, the day for my quarterly salary was coming up. As usual, I was praying a lot about it. The day
arrived. My friend didn't mention my salary. I kept
praying. Days went by. He didn't remember. Finally
one Saturday night I was doing my accounts for the
week and discovered I only had a ten pence piece left.
Well, I hadn't needed anything yet, so I kept praying.

That Sunday was really great. As usual, my heart
brimmed over with the feeling of being blessed. After
church in the morning, my afternoons and evenings
were full of gospel work at the rooming houses I usual-

ly visited. They were in the poorest part of town. At times like that, it felt almost as if heaven had begun to exist on earth. It didn't seem like I needed a better idea of what joy was. I just needed more capacity to appreciate it.

I finished my last service at about ten o'clock that night. Afterwards, a poor man asked me to go pray with his wife. He told me she was dying. I agreed without hesitation. On the way to his house, I asked him why he hadn't sent for the priest. His accent told me he was an Irishman.

"I did," he said. "But the priest refused to come unless I paid seven pence." The family was starving, and the man didn't have the money.

Immediately I thought about the one coin I had, a single ten pence coin. I usually had a bowl of watery cereal for supper. I knew it already waited for me at home. And I had enough for breakfast the next morning. But I didn't have anything for dinner the next day.

Instantly the joy stopped flowing. But instead of scolding myself, I began to scold the poor man. I told him he was wrong to let things get so bad. He should have gone to the officer in charge of relief.

"I did," he said. They had told him to come at eleven o'clock the next morning. But he was afraid his wife might not live through the night.

I thought, If only I had a five pence piece and five pennies instead of this ten pence coin! I'd gladly give these poor folks the five pence! But I didn't think of giving up the ten pence. It was as if I could trust God and a little money, but I wasn't ready to trust him alone—without any money at all. But I just didn't see it.

The man led me into a courtyard. Nervously I followed him down it. I'd been there before. The last time I visited there I'd been harassed. My tracts had been torn to pieces and I'd been warned not to come back, so I felt rather worried.

I was on the path of duty, though. So I followed on. He led me up a miserable flight of stairs and into a dismal room. What a sight! Four or five children stood around. Their faces were skin and bone. They told an obvious story: slow starvation. An exhausted mother lay on a mattress with a tiny baby, just thirty-six hours old. Instead of crying, the baby moaned. It was probably dying, too.

If I had a five and a five pennies instead of a ten pence coin, I thought, I'd be glad to give them the five pence and two ones! I felt an inner push to help them by giving them everything I had. But even now, unbelief kept me from obeying it.

Of course I couldn't say much to comfort the poor people. I needed comfort myself. I began to tell them not to be discouraged, even though their circumstances were terrible, because there was a kind and loving Father in heaven.

"You hypocrite!" something inside me said. "Telling these unsaved people about a kind, loving Father in heaven when you're not ready to trust him yourself. Unless you have ten pence!" I nearly choked.

I would have gladly compromised my conscience if

I had owned a five pence piece and five pennies! I would have gladly given up eight pence and kept two pennies. But I still wasn't ready to trust God alone—without anything.

Under the circumstances, it was impossible to talk. Well, I won't have any trouble praying, I thought. I loved praying. It never seemed tiring or boring. I never ran out of words. I honestly thought I could just kneel down and start praying. They'd get relief, and I'd get it at the same time. "You asked me to come pray with your wife," I said to the man. "Let's pray."

I knelt down. I'd barely opened my mouth with, "Our Father who art in heaven" when my conscience spoke inside me. "Do you dare to mock God? Do you dare to kneel down and call him Father with ten pence in your pocket?"

Before or since, I have never experienced so much inner conflict. I have no idea how I got through that form prayer. I don't know whether the words were connected or not. I got up from my knees in turmoil.

The poor father turned to me. "You see what a terrible state we're in, sir," he said. "If you can help us, for God's sake, do!'

Just then the words flashed into my mind, "Give to everyone who asks you" (Luke 6:30).

There is power in the King's word. I put my hand in my pocket and slowly pulled out the ten pence coin. I handed it to the man. "It might seem trivial for me to help you," I told him. "You can see I'm comparatively well off. But when I gave up that coin, I gave you all I had."

I had been trying to tell him the truth. God really was a Father. He really could be trusted. The joy flooded back into my heart. Finally, I could talk and really mean it. The problem that hindered blessing was gone, hopefully forever.

It wasn't just the poor woman's life that was saved. I realized my life was saved, too. I would have been a wreck as a Christian if grace hadn't conquered me then. If I hadn't obeyed God's Spirit.

As I went home to my apartment that night, my heart felt as light as my pocket. The lonely, deserted streets rang with a praise song I couldn't hold back. When I ate my bowl of cereal before going to bed, I wouldn't have exchanged it for a prince's feast.

As I knelt by my bed, I reminded the Lord of his own word: that "he who is kind to the poor lends to the Lord" (Prov. 19:17). "Don't let my loan be a long one," I asked, "or I won't have any dinner tomorrow."

With peace inside and out I spent a happy, restful night.

The next morning for breakfast, I still had a plate of oatmeal. But before I ate it, I heard the postman knock at the door. Usually, I didn't get any letters on Monday. That was because my parents and most of my friends didn't send mail on Saturday. So I was a bit surprised when the landlady came in holding a letter in her wet hand.

I looked at the letter. I didn't recognize the handwriting. It was either someone I didn't know, or someone had purposely changed their writing. The postmark was blurry. I couldn't figure out where it came from.

When I opened the envelope, I found a pair of kid gloves folded inside a blank sheet of paper. Surprised, I opened the gloves. Forty pence fell on the floor.

"Praise the Lord!" I exclaimed, "Four hundred percent for twelve hours' investment! That's good interest. The Hull businessmen would be glad if they could lend their money at that rate!"

Right then and there, I decided that a bank that couldn't break would have my savings—and earnings. I've never regretted the decision.

I can't tell you how often I've thought about this incident. It's been a great help to me during difficult times. If we're faithful to God in little things, we'll grow in experience and gain strength that will help us in life's more serious trials.

CHAPTER FOUR

FURTHER ANSWERS TO PRAYER

THIS AMAZING ANSWER TO PRAYER gave me a lot of joy. It also strengthened my faith. But even if I stretched the money as far as I could, it wouldn't last long. I had to continue praying that my employer would remember and pay my wages.

All my requests seemed unanswered. Before two weeks passed, I found myself in pretty much the same situation as before. Meanwhile, I pleaded with God, more and more earnestly all the time. Lord, remind my boss that my salary is overdue.

It wasn't actually not having money that upset me. I could have gotten it any time. If I asked. The question in my mind was, "Can I go to China? Or will my lack of faith be too big of an obstacle? Will it keep me from becoming a missionary?"

As the week ended, I felt really embarrassed. I didn't just have myself to think about. My Saturday night payment was due to my landlady, a Christian. I knew she couldn't do without it. For her sake, shouldn't I say something about my salary?

To do that, I felt, would be to admit I wasn't up to being a missionary. Instead of working Thursday and Friday, I spent most of the time wrestling with God in prayer. Saturday morning I was still in the same position.

Now I asked for guidance. Should I break my silence and tell my employer? Or should I keep waiting for the Father's time? As far as I could tell, God assured me it was best to wait for his time. In some way or other, he would take care of my need. So, I waited. My heart now rested, the burden was gone.

About five o'clock Saturday afternoon, the doctor finished writing prescriptions. His last visits for the day were done. As usual, he threw himself down in his armchair. He began to talk about God. The doctor was a true Christian. We'd had many times of happy spiritual fellowship together.

I was busy, watching a boiling prescription that needed a lot of attention. That was a good thing. Without any obvious connection to what was going on, he suddenly said, "By the way, Taylor, isn't your salary due again?"

You can imagine my feelings! I had to swallow two or three times before I could speak. I kept my eyes fixed on the pan and my back to the doctor. As quietly as I could, I told him my salary was overdue.

At that moment, thankfulness flooded me! God had heard my prayer. My employer had remembered the salary just when I needed it so much. Without a word from me.

"Oh, I'm sorry you didn't remind me!" he said. "You

know how busy I am. I wish I'd thought of it sooner. I sent all the money I had to the bank this afternoon, or I'd pay you now."

I can't describe my horror. I didn't know what to do. Fortunately, my pan almost boiled over and I had to rush it out of the room. I was glad to get away. I kept out of sight until the doctor went home. Thankfully, he didn't notice I was upset.

As soon as he left, I went to my quiet place and poured out my heart before the Lord for a while. Finally, calmness returned. Even better, thankfulness and joy came. God has his own way. He wasn't going to fail me.

Earlier that day, I had asked him what he wanted. As far as I could tell, he had said to wait patiently. God was going to help me some other way.

As usual on a Saturday, I spent the evening reading the Bible and getting ready to speak at the different lodging houses the next day. Maybe I waited a little longer than usual. No interruptions.

Finally, at ten o'clock I put on my coat and got ready to go home. Actually, I was thankful I would have to let myself in. My landlady went to bed early. Nothing could possibly come that night, but maybe God would do something for me by Monday. If I'd had the money, I would have given it to her before now.

Just as I was about to turn down the gas, I heard the doctor walking in the garden. It stood between the house and the surgery building. He was laughing, as though he found something really funny. He came into the surgery and asked for the ledger. One of his richest patients had just come to pay his doctor's bill, he told me. Wasn't that odd?

It never hit me that it might have anything to do with me, or I might have felt embarrassed. I just looked at it from the perspective of a spectator. It was rather funny. A man rolling in money came after ten o'clock at night to pay his doctor's bill when he could easily have paid it any day with a check. For some reason, he couldn't rest with this bill on his mind. He'd just had to come at that strange hour to pay what he owed.

The account was entered in the ledger and the doctor was about to leave. Suddenly, he turned. Handing me some of the notes he'd just received, he said, "By the way, Taylor, you might as well take these notes. I don't have any change, but I can give you the rest next week."

He left without realizing how it affected me. Surprised and thankful, I went back to my private space to praise God. My heart was joyful. I might get to China after all!

To me, this incident was not trivial. Sometimes I think about it when things get really difficult. In China, and elsewhere, it has comforted and strengthened me a lot.

The time finally came for me to leave Hull to study medicine at the London Hospital. I had every reason to expect that after a little while there I would begin my life's work in China. I rejoiced that God was willing to hear and answer prayer, and to help me, his half-trusting, half-timid child. But I still felt I couldn't go to

China without more growth and testing in my ability to rest in his faithfulness.

Then an obvious opportunity for more growth came along.

My dear father had offered to cover all the expenses for my stay in London. I knew, though, that he'd had some recent losses. It would mean a big sacrifice for him to do it right then, although it seemed the time for me to go.

I had recently gotten acquainted with the committee of the Chinese Evangelization Society. They were the group I would eventually go to China with. I had especially gotten to know its secretary, Mr. George Pearse, a friend I love and admire. At the time he was with the Stock Exchange, but has been a missionary for many years now.

The committee didn't know about my father's offer. They also offered to cover my expenses while I was in London. When I first got the offer, I wasn't sure what to do. I wrote both to the society's secretaries and to my father and told them I would take a few days to pray about it before deciding what to do. To my father, I mentioned the society's offer, and also I told the secretaries about my father's proposal.

While I waited on God, I realized I could easily refuse both offers. The society's secretaries wouldn't know I had thrown myself completely on God for support. My father would conclude that I had accepted the other offer. So I wrote, declining both proposals. Without anyone worrying about me, I was simply in

God's hands. He knew my heart. If he wanted to encourage me to go to China, he would bless my effort to now try depending only on him.

C H A P T E R   F I V E

LIFE IN LONDON

I WON'T GO INTO THE WAYS GOD helped me every now and then. It was usually to my surprise and delight. I quickly learned I couldn't live as inexpensively in London as I could in Hull. To cut expenses, I shared a room with a cousin who lived four miles from the hospital.

I paid for my own food. The cheapest way to live, I found, was to eat brown bread and water most of the time. This way, I could make the money God gave me last as long as possible. Some expenses I couldn't cut down on, but I could control my board. I bought a large two penny loaf of brown bread on my long walk from the hospital. It gave me supper and breakfast. On that diet, with a few apples for lunch, I managed to walk eight or nine miles a day. In addition to that, it kept me going when I was on my feet at the hospital and medical school.

I have to mention one thing that happened. The husband of my former landlady in Hull was the chief officer of a ship that sailed out of London. By collecting half his pay every month, and sending it to her, I could save her the cost of doing so. I'd been doing this several months when she wrote asking me to get the next payment as early as possible. Her rent was almost due and she needed that money to pay it.

The request came at an inconvenient time. I was working hard, studying for an exam. I hoped to get a scholarship, and didn't feel I could afford the time to go to the city and get the money during the busiest part of the day. I had enough of my own money with me, so I sent the amount she needed. As soon as the exam was over, I would go get her regular allowance to reimburse what I'd paid out.

The medical school closed for a day just before exam time because of the Duke of Wellington's funeral, so I was able to go to the office right away and ask for the money. It was located on a street just outside Cheapside. To my surprise and dismay, the clerk told me he couldn't pay it. The woman's husband had run away from his ship and gone to dig gold.

"Well," I said, "that's rather inconvenient! I already advanced the money. I know his wife won't be able to repay me."

The clerk said he was sorry, but he had to obey orders. He couldn't help me.

After thinking a while, it comforted me to remember I depended on the Lord for everything. He wasn't broke. It was no big deal for him if I needed more money a little sooner than normal. I didn't go without joy and peace for long.

Soon after this, possibly that evening, I was sewing some sheets of paper together. I would use them to take lecture notes. I accidentally pricked the first finger of my right hand, but forgot all about it in a few minutes.

The next day at the hospital, I continued dissecting as before. The body was of someone who had died of fever and was more disgusting and dangerous than usual. Those of us working on it were especially careful because we knew the slightest scratch could cost us our lives.

Before much time had gone by, I began to feel extremely tired. As I walked through the surgical wards at noon, I had to run out because I suddenly got very sick. This was unusual for me since I ate very little—nothing that could upset my stomach. For a while, I felt faint. Then a drink of cold water revived me and I was able to rejoin the other students.

But I got sicker and sicker. Before the afternoon lecture on surgery finished, I lost my ability to hold the pencil and take notes. By the time the next lecture ended, pain riddled my whole arm and right side. I looked and felt sick.

I couldn't start work again, so I went to the dissecting room to cover up the section I'd been working on and put away the apparatus. "I can't think what's come over me," I told the demonstrator, who was a skilled surgeon.

When I described the symptoms, he said, "It's clear enough what happened. You must have cut yourself while you were dissecting. You know this is a case of malignant fever."

I assured him I'd been very careful. I was absolutely sure I had no cut or scratch.

"Well," he replied, "you have to have one." He scrutinized my hand, but couldn't find it.

Suddenly it occurred to me. I had pricked my finger the night before! "Is it possible that a prick from a needle last night could have still been open?" I asked.

"Ah, that's probably it," he answered. He advised me to get a cab. "Get home as fast as you can, and settle your affairs immediately," he said. "Because you're a dead man."

My first thought was sad: I wouldn't be able to go to China. But soon another feeling came. "Unless I'm totally wrong, I have work to do in China. I'm not going to die."

Actually, I was glad for the opportunity to talk to my medical friend. He was a confirmed skeptic when it came to spiritual things. I told him about the joy I had when I thought about being with my Master soon. "But I don't think I'll die," I said. "Unless I'm completely mistaken, I have work in China to do. So, no matter what the struggle is, I have to get through this."

"That's fine," he answered, "but get a cab and drive home as fast as you can. You don't have any time to lose. You'll soon be incapable of winding things up."

I smiled a little at the idea of going home in a cab. By this time, I didn't have enough money for that! I set out to walk the distance, if I could. Before long my strength gave out. There was no use trying to reach home by walking.

Taking a bus from Whitechapel Church to Farringdon Street, and another from Farringdon on, I reached the Soho Square neighborhood, in front of where I lived. I suffered a lot. I went into the house and I got some hot water from the servant. As I took it, I told her to accept eternal life as God's gift through Jesus Christ. I said it earnestly, literally like a dying man. Then I washed my head and lanced the finger, hoping to let out some of the poisoned blood. The pain was extreme and I fainted.

I was unconscious so long that when I woke up I discovered I'd been carried to bed.

An uncle, who lived nearby, had come in and sent for his own doctor, an assistant surgeon at the Westminster Hospital. I assured my uncle that medical help wouldn't do me much good. Besides, I didn't want to have to pay for it.

He told me not to worry. Since he'd sent for his own doctor, he'd get the bill.

When the surgeon came and learned what had happened, he said, "Well, if you've been living moderately, you might pull through. But if you've been indulging in beer and stuff like that, you haven't got a chance."

If sober living can help, few people would have a better chance than I do, I thought. I had eaten hardly anything but bread and water for a long time. I told him I had eaten very sparingly. I found it helped me study.

"But now," he said, "you have to keep up your strength. It's going to be a pretty hard struggle." He prescribed a bottle of port wine every day, and as many chops as I could eat.

Again, I smiled inwardly. I had no way to buy such luxuries! My kind uncle took care of this problem, though. He immediately sent me everything I needed.

In spite of the agony I suffered, I was worried. My dear parents might hear about my situation. Some time in thought and prayer satisfied me that I wasn't going to die. In fact, I knew God had work for me to do in China. But if my parents came and found me so sick, I'd lose the opportunity to see how God was going to work for me, since my money had almost run out.

After praying for guidance, I got my uncle and cousin to promise not to write my parents. I would communicate with them myself. When they gave me their word, I felt it was a distinct answer to prayer. I was careful to leave all communication with my parents until the crisis had passed. At home they knew I was working hard, preparing for an exam, and didn't wonder about my silence.

Days and nights of suffering passed slowly. Finally, after several weeks, I was well enough to leave my room. That was when I learned that two men from a different hospital had gotten dissection wounds at the same time I did. Both had died. But God spared me to work in China, in answer to prayer.

CHAPTER SIX

STRENGTHENED BY FAITH

ONE DAY THE DOCTOR CAME IN AND found me on the sofa. He was surprised to learn I'd walked downstairs with help. "Now," he said, "the best thing you can do is go to the country as soon as you feel up to traveling. You need to stay there until you've recovered enough health and strength. If you start work again too soon, there will be serious consequences."

After he left, I lay on the sofa, exhausted, and told the Lord all about it. "Lord, you know I'm not telling anyone about my needs. Especially anyone likely to want to help. Strengthen my faith by giving me your help in answer to prayer alone. And show me what to do." Then I waited for his answer.

He seemed to direct my mind to the idea of going to the shipping office again, to ask about the wages I hadn't been able to get back. I reminded the Lord I couldn't afford to take a bus or taxi. It didn't seem likely that I would get the money anyway. "Is this impulse just grasping at straws?" I asked. Maybe it was all in my head, not his guidance and teaching. But after prayer, and more waiting on God, I felt reassured. God himself was telling me to go to the office.

My next question was, "How can I go?" I'd needed help coming downstairs. The shipping office was at least two miles away.

The assurance came vividly. Whatever I asked God in Christ's name he would do, so that the Father would be glorified in the Son. I needed to seek strength for the long walk, to receive it by faith, and to set out.

Without hesitation I told the Lord, "I'm perfectly willing to take the walk if you give me the strength." In the name of Christ, I asked that he would strengthen me immediately. Then I sent the servant up to my room for my hat and stick. I set out, not to try to walk, but to walk to Cheapside.

Faith definitely strengthened me. But I've never taken as much interest in shop windows as I did on that trip! Every second or third step, I was glad I could lean against the plate glass and examine the window's contents for a few seconds. Then I passed on.

It took an extra effort of faith when I got to the bottom of Farringdon Street and had to face the tiresome climb up Snow Hill. There was no Holborn Viaduct in those days, so I had to climb the hill. God helped me incredibly. Finally, I reached Cheapside and turned onto the side street where the office was located. I sat down, exhausted, on the steps leading to the second floor office where I was headed.

I felt awkward sitting there on the steps, obviously

worn out. The men who rushed up and down the stairs eyed me with curiosity. After a short rest and more prayer, I managed to climb the stairs. Thankfully, the clerk I'd dealt with before was in the office. I must have looked pale and exhausted, so he asked about my health. I told him I'd had a serious illness and had been told to go to the country. "But I thought I should come in first, and check one more time, just in case there had been a mistake and the mate didn't really run off to dig gold."

"Oh," he said, "I'm so glad you came. It turns out that the one who ran away was an able seaman with the same name. The mate is still on board. The ship has just reached Gravesend, and will arrive here very soon. But I'm happy to pay you half his wages up to this point. I'm sure it'll reach his wife more safely through you. We all know what temptations the men have when they arrive home after a voyage."

Before giving me the money, he insisted I come inside and share his lunch. The Lord was certainly providing for me! I accepted his offer with a thankful heart.

When I felt refreshed and rested, he gave me a sheet of paper. "Write a few lines to the wife," he said, "and tell her the situation." On my way back, I stopped in Cheapside and bought a money order for the balance due to her and mailed it. By now, I felt quite justified in taking a bus as far as it would take me towards home.

The next morning, after taking care of some business, I felt a lot better. I headed for the office of the doctor who had taken care of me. My uncle planned to pay the bill, but I thought the right thing for me to do was to settle the account myself, since I had money now. The kind surgeon refused to let me pay anything for his services because I was a medical student. He did let me pay forty pence for the quinine he'd given me.

When that was settled, I noticed that the amount left was just enough to take me home. What a wonderful way God had intervened for me!

I knew the surgeon was skeptical. I told him I wanted to talk freely to him, if I could do it without offending him. "Under God, I owe my life to your kind care," I said, "and I honestly wish you would benefit from the same faith I have.

I told him my reason for being in London, and described my situation. I told him I hadn't accepted my father's help. I hadn't accepted the help of the officers at the mission agency I'd probably to go China with, either. I told the recent story of how God had provided for me. The day before, when he had ordered me to go to the country, my position had been hopeless—unless I told somebody what I needed. But I was determined not to. Then I described the mental exercises I had gone through.

When I told him I'd actually gotten up and walked to Cheapside, he looked at me as if he didn't believe me. "Impossible! I left you lying there more like a ghost than a man."

I had to assure him over and over that I really had taken the walk, strengthened by faith. I also told him about the money I had left and what I still had to pay.

Then I showed him I had just enough to take me home to Yorkshire, including food along the way and the bus ride at the end.

My kind friend was completely broken down. "I would give all the world for a faith like yours," he said with tears in his eyes.

I had the joy of telling him he could get it without money or price.

We never met again. When my health and strength were restored and I returned to town, I learned he'd had a stroke and had gone to the country. Later, I learned he never recovered. I couldn't find out anything about his state of mind when he died, but I've always been thankful I had the opportunity to tell him about the Lord, and took it. I have to hope that the Master himself spoke to him through me. And that I'll meet him again in heaven. What joy to be welcomed by him when my own time is over!

The next day I was in my dear parents' home. I had too much joy because of the Lord's help and deliverance to keep the story to myself. Before I returned to London, my dear mother knew the secrets I had kept a long time. Needless to say, when I went back to town again, I wasn't allowed to live as cheaply as I had before. I couldn't have lived that way anyway. I needed more now, and the Lord provided it.

CHAPTER SEVEN

MIGHTY TO SAVE

WHEN I WAS ENOUGH BETTER, I
returned to London to start studying again, back to the
busy hospital and lecture hall life. This was often
relieved by happy Sundays, meeting with Christian
friends, especially in London or Tottenham.
Opportunities to serve are everywhere. My life was no
exception. I'll just mention one case that really encouraged me to expect people to get converted even when it
seemed hopeless.

God had given me the joy of winning souls before,
but not where it was especially hard. Everything is possible with God. And no conversion ever takes place
except with the Holy Spirit's almighty power. So,
what's really needed is for every Christian worker to
know God. In fact, that's why he gave us eternal life.
Our Savior himself said it in a verse which is often
quoted wrong. John 17:3 says, "Now this is [the object
of] eternal life [not to know but] that they may know
you, the only true God, and Jesus Christ, whom you
have sent."

I was about to prove how willing God is to answer prayer for spiritual blessing when it just doesn't seem likely at all. I would get better acquainted with the prayer-answering God as someone "mighty to save."

A little while before I left for China, I got the daily job of dressing the foot of a patient with gangrene. The disease started, as usual, without seeming so terrible. The patient had no idea he was doomed. He probably thought he had a long time to live.

I wasn't the first person to take care of him, but when the case was transferred to me, I naturally got rather anxious about his soul. He lived with a Christian family. From them I learned he was an avowed atheist, and very antagonistic to anything religious.

Without asking if it was okay with him, they had invited someone to come read scripture to him. In a great passion, he had ordered him from the room. A vicar from the district also visited, hoping to help the man, but he had spit in his face. He refused to let the vicar speak to him. I heard he had a violent temper. As you can imagine, the case seemed hopeless.

I prayed about it a lot when I first started taking care of him. For two or three days, though, I didn't say anything to him that would sound religious. By dressing his diseased leg with extra care, I was able to cut his suffering down considerably. Soon he began to show grateful appreciation for what I did for him. One day, with my heart in my mouth, I took advantage of his friendly words to tell him why I acted the way I did. I also told him about his own rather serious position and that he needed God's mercy through Christ.

Only with great effort did he keep his mouth shut. He turned over in bed with his back to me and didn't say a word.

I couldn't get the poor man out of my mind. Often, throughout the day, I pleaded with God, by his Spirit, to save the man before he died. After dressing the wound and relieving the man's pain, I always said a few words to him, and hoped the Lord would bless them. He always turned his back to me, looking annoyed. But he never said a word in reply.

This went on for quite a while, and my heart sank. Not only did it seem to be doing no good. It might even be hardening him and increasing his guilt. One day, after dressing his leg and washing my hands, instead of going back to the bed to talk to him, I went to the door. For a few seconds, I hesitated. "Ephraim is joined to idols," I thought, "leave him alone!" (Hosea 4:17).

I looked at the man and saw his surprise. It was the first time since I had first spoken to him about the Lord that I had tried to leave without going to his bedside and saying a few words for my Master. I couldn't bear it any longer. Bursting into tears, I crossed the room. "My friend," I said, "whether you hear or not, I have to take care of my own soul." I continued, speaking earnestly. With many tears I told him how much I wanted him to let me pray with him.

I felt indescribable joy when he didn't turn away. Instead he said, "Go ahead, if it will make you feel better."

Obviously, I fell on my knees and poured my heart out to God for him. I believe God worked a change in his soul right then and there.

After that, he never acted reluctant to let me speak to him and pray with him. Within a few days, he definitely accepted Christ as his Savior. It gave me incredible joy to see the dear man rejoicing in the hope of God's glory!

He told me that for forty years, he hadn't darkened a church or chapel door. Even then, forty years ago, he had only entered a place of worship to get married. And they hadn't persuaded him to go inside when his wife was buried.

Now, thank God, I had every reason to believe that his sin-stained soul was washed, sanctified and justified in the name of the Lord Jesus Christ, and in God's Spirit. Often during my early work in China, circumstances made me feel almost hopeless. Then I thought about this man's conversion. It encouraged me to keep on speaking the Word, whether people heard or not.

Now happy, even though he was suffering, this man lived some time after his conversion. He never got tired of giving his testimony of God's grace. His condition was really distressing. But the change in his character and behavior made what had been a painful duty into a real pleasure. Since then, I have often thought of the words, "He who goes out weeping, carrying seed to sow, will return with songs of joy, carrying sheaves with him" (Psalm 126:6). Maybe if we had more of that intense distress for souls, so that we actually cried, we would see the results we long for more often. Sometimes when we complain about how hard people's hearts are, we may fail because of the hardness of our own hearts, and because of our own feeble understanding of the importance of eternal things.

CHAPTER EIGHT

VOYAGE TO CHINA

SOON THE TIME I'D BEEN WAITING for so long arrived. It was time to leave England for China. Before I left, many people prayed over me for the ministry I would have, giving God's word to the unbelieving Chinese. I left London for Liverpool.

On September 19, 1853, a little service took place in the stern cabin of the *Dumfries*. The Chinese Evangelization Society, which I would represent in China, had booked the cabin for me.

My dear mother, who is now in heaven, had come to see me off in Liverpool. I will never forget that day. And I won't forget how she accompanied me into the little cabin that would be my home for nearly six long months. With a mother's loving hand, she smoothed the little bed. She sat beside me and joined in the last hymn we would sing together for a long time. We knelt, and she prayed—the last mother's prayer I would hear before leaving for China. We were told it was time for her to leave the ship. We said goodbye never expecting to see each other on earth again.

For my sake, she held her feelings in as much as she could. She went on shore, giving me her blessing. I stood alone on deck, and she followed the ship as it moved toward the dock gates. As we passed through the gates, and the separation really began, I will never forget the cry of anguish that burst from my mother's heart. It went through me like a knife. Until then, I never knew so completely what "God so loved the world" meant. And I am quite sure my dear mother learned more about God's love for the lost at that time than in her whole life up to that point.

It must really grieve God's heart when he sees his children so indifferent to the needs of the wide world—for which his dearly loved and only Son died.

> Listen, O daughter, consider and give ear:
>   Forget your people and your father's house.
> The king is enthralled by your beauty;
>   honor him, for he is your lord.
> (Psalm 45:10)

Praise God, more and more people are finding out about the joy and the wonderful revelation of his mercy which he gives to those who follow him! Emptying themselves, they are leaving everything to obey his great commission.

On September 19, 1853, the *Dumfries* sailed into China, but I didn't arrive in Shanghai until March 1, in the spring of the following year.

Our voyage started rough, but many people had

promised to pray constantly for us. It really helped to know this. We had barely left the Mersey when a violent gale caught us. For twelve days, we tacked backwards and forwards in the Irish Channel, unable to get out to sea. The gale steadily increased. For almost a week we held the ship stationary in the wind. But we were on a lee coast. We had to set sail again, so we tried to tack into the wind.

The greatest efforts of the captain and crew didn't help. Sunday night, September 25, found us drifting into Carnarvon Bay. Every time we tested the depth, it was shallower. Finally we were within a stone's throw of the rocks. The ship refused to stop.

About this time, as they turned the ship in the other direction, the Christian captain said, "In half an hour we'll be dead. What about your call to work for the Lord in China?"

I had already gone through some inner conflict, but it was over. I felt tremendously joyful and was happy to tell him I wouldn't be anywhere else for anything in the world. I definitely expected to reach China. But if not, my Master would be able to say I'd been trying to obey his call.

Within a few minutes of putting up a flag, the captain walked up to the compass. "The wind has freed two points," he told me. "We'll be able to tack out of the bay." And we did.

The bowsprit [on the front of the boat] was cracking and the vessel was seriously strained. But in a few days we made it out to sea. The needed repairs were done so completely on board that we made our journey to China without a problem.

One thing really bothered me that night, though. I was a very young believer. I didn't have enough faith in God to see that he worked in and through things I could use to help myself.

I had felt obligated to give in to something my mother really wanted. For her sake, I had bought a life vest. But in my own soul, I felt that as long as I had the life vest, I wasn't trusting in God alone. My heart didn't have any rest until that night, when I gave it away— after all hope of being saved was gone. Then I had perfect peace. The funny thing is, I put together several light things which were likely to float. That didn't bother me at all. And I didn't feel like I was being inconsistent either.

Ever since then I have clearly seen the mistake I was making. It is a very common mistake these days, when false teaching on faith healing does so much harm. This teaching misleads some in regard to God's purposes, and shakes the faith of others, and upsets many. Using things and methods to help ourselves shouldn't lessen our faith in God. And our faith in God shouldn't keep us from using whatever method he gives us to accomplish his purposes.

For years after this, I always took a life vest with me. It never bothered me. This is because after the storm passed, a prayerful Bible study settled the question for me. God showed me my mistake, probably to keep me from a lot of trouble about similar questions that come up so often now.

When I've been in charge of any case, medical or surgical, I've never considered the idea of not asking for God's guidance and blessing as I used the instrument I needed. And I've never failed to thank him for answered prayer and restored health. To me, it seems presumptuous and wrong to not use the help he has put in our reach. It would be the same as not eating every day, as if prayer alone can maintain life and health.

The journey was incredibly tedious. We lost a lot of time at the equator because of no wind. When we finally reached the Eastern Archipelago we had the same problem again. Usually, a breeze would come up after sunset and last almost until dawn. They made the best of it. But during the day we lay still in the water, sails flapping. In fact, we often drifted backwards and lost a lot of the advantage we'd gotten during the night.

This happened one time when we were dangerously near northern New Guinea. Saturday night had brought us to a point thirty miles off shore. During the Sunday service on deck, I couldn't help noticing that the captain looked worried. And he kept going over to the side of the ship.

When the service ended, he told me why. A four-knot current was carrying us rapidly toward some sunken reefs. We were already so near that it seemed as though we probably wouldn't make it through the afternoon. After lunch, they put out the longboat. All hands tried, unsuccessfully, to turn the ship away from the shore.

For a while we stood together on deck in silence. Then the captain said to me, "Well, we've done everything we can do. We just have to wait."

Then something occurred to me. "No," I replied, "there is one thing we haven't done yet."

"What's that?" he asked.

"Four of us on board are Christians," I answered. The four were the Swedish carpenter, our steward, the captain and myself. "Let's all go to our cabins," I went on, "to pray in agreement, asking the Lord to give us a breeze immediately. He can send it now just as easily as at sunset."

The captain agreed, and I went and talked to the other two men. After praying with the carpenter, all four of us went in to wait on God. I had a good but very short prayer time. I felt so satisfied that God had granted our request that I couldn't keep on asking. Soon I went up on deck again. The first officer, a godless man, was in charge. I went over and asked him to let down the corners of the mainsail. They had been pulled up to cut down on the useless flapping of the sail against the rigging.

"What would be the good of that?" he asked.

I told him we'd been asking God to give us a wind, that it was coming immediately, and that we were so near to the reef by this time, there wasn't any time to lose.

He gave me a look of incredulity and contempt. He swore and said he'd rather see a wind than hear about it! But while he was speaking I watched his eye and followed it up the royal [topmost sail]. There, sure enough, the corner of the sail began to tremble in the coming breeze.

"Don't you see the wind coming? Look at the royal!" I exclaimed.

"No, it's only a cat's paw [a mere puff of wind]," he answered.

"Cat's paw or not," I said, "please let down the mainsail so we can benefit from it!"

He was slow to do it. In another minute, the heavy tread of men on deck brought the captain from his cabin. He came to see what was the matter and saw that the breeze had come. In a few minutes we were plowing along at six or seven knots through the water. We were soon out of danger. Though the wind was sometimes unsteady, we didn't lose it completely until after passing the Pelew Islands.

This is the way God encouraged me, before I landed on China's shores, to bring everything to him in prayer. And to expect him to honor Jesus' name and give the help needed in each emergency.

CHAPTER NINE

EARLY MISSIONARY EXPERIENCES

AFTER LANDING IN SHANGHAI ON March 1, 1854, I found myself surrounded by completely unexpected problems. A band of rebels, known as the "Red Turbans," had taken over the part of the city where the Chinese lived. An imperial army was encamped against them—from forty to fifty thousand men. They caused more discomfort and danger to the little European community than the rebels did.

I was told it was impossible to live outside the Settlement [the international settlement under European control, which lasted from 1843-1943]. But in the foreign areas, you could hardly get an apartment at any price. The dollar, which is now worth about fifteen pence, had risen to a value of forty-four pence. With only a small income in English money, my prospects weren't very good.

I did have three letters of introduction. I especially counted on getting advice and help from one man I'd been sent to because I knew and respected his friends. Of course, I looked for him right away. I learned he'd been buried a month or two before. He had died from fever while I had sailed from England.

The news made me sad, but I asked about another missionary I had a letter of introduction for. More disappointment. He'd gone to America.

I still had the third letter, but someone I hardly knew had given it to me. I had expected less from it than from the other two. It turned out to be God's channel of help. It was addressed to Dr. Medhurst, of the London Mission [London Missionary Society]. He introduced me to Dr. Lockhart, who was kind enough to let me live with him for six months. Dr. Medhurst got me my first Chinese teacher, and he, along with Dr. Edkins, and Mr. Alexander Wylie gave me a lot of help with the language.

They were troublesome times, though. And dangerous. One day I was leaving the city with Mr. Wylie. He started to talk to two coolies. We were waiting at the East Gate for someone coming behind us. Before our companion caught up, an attack on the city began. It came from the batteries on the other side of the river. It made us hurry off to find a safer place since cannon balls were whizzing uncomfortably close to us.

Unfortunately, the coolies stayed too long, and were wounded.

When we reached the Settlement, we stopped a few minutes to buy something. Then we went immediately to the London Mission compound. There, at the hospital door, we found the poor coolies Mr. Wylie had been talking with. A cannon ball had shattered their ankles.

The poor men refused amputation and both died. What a narrow escape we'd had!

At another time, early in the morning, I joined one of the missionaries on his porch to watch how the battle went. We were about three quarters of a mile away. Suddenly, a spent ball passed by between us and buried itself in the porch wall.

Another day, after lunch, my friend Mr. Wylie left a book on the table. When he came back to get it five minutes later, he found the arm of the chair he'd been sitting in blown completely away. But in the middle of these and many other dangerous situations, God protected us.

After staying with Dr. Lockhart for six months, I rented a native house outside the Settlement. I started to do a little missionary work among my Chinese neighbors. This was only possible for a few more months.

When the French joined the Imperialist attack on the city, there began to be skirmishes every night. My house's location became so dangerous that during the last few weeks I gave up trying to sleep except during the day.

One night a fire looked really close. I climbed up to a small observation deck I'd made on the roof. I wanted to see if I needed to try and escape. While I was there, a cannon ball hit the ridge of the roof on the opposite side of the quadrangle. Broken pieces of tile showered down all around me. The ball itself rolled down into the court below. It weighed four or five pounds. If it had come a few inches higher, it probably would have hit me instead of the building. My mother kept that ball for many years.

A little later, I had to abandon the house and return to the foreign Settlement. My move wasn't any too soon. Before the last of my things had been taken out of the house, it burned to the ground.

It's hard to give an adequate idea of how hard this early period was. To someone sensitive, the horrors, atrocities and misery connected with war were a terrible ordeal. It was also very embarrassing at times. I had an income of only eighty pounds a year. When I moved into the Settlement, I had to give a hundred and twenty for rent, and sublet half the house. After Dr. Parker arrived and they learned more about our situation, the committee of the Chinese Evangelization Society raised my income. But by then I'd already had many painful experiences.

Few people would understand how distressing these problems seemed to someone so young and inexperienced. Or how intensely lonely it was, since I couldn't even hint about what I was going through. To do that would have been like asking for help.

The Enemy is always ready with the idea he repeats so often: "All these things are against you."

What a lie! The cold, even the hunger, the times of watching, the sleepless nights of danger, and the feelings I had when I was alone and helpless were chosen well and wisely. They were tenderly and lovingly handed out. What else could have made God's word seem that sweet? Or his presence so real? Or his help so precious?

They were times of emptying and humbling. But I wasn't ashamed of those experiences. They strengthened my purpose to go forward as God directed, with his proved promise, "I will never leave you nor forsake you" (Joshua 1:5).

Even now that things have gotten a lot easier for missionaries I can see and rejoice that "as for God, his way is perfect" (2 Samuel 22:31).

CHAPTER TEN

FIRST EVANGELISTIC EFFORTS

TRAVELING INLAND WAS AGAINST the rules of the treaties. It was also very difficult. This was especially true for quite a while after the battle of Muddy Flat, where an Anglo-American contingent of about three hundred marines and seamen, along with a volunteer corps of less than a hundred residents, attacked the Imperial camp. They drove from 30,000 to 50,000 Chinese soldiers away because the range of our shot and shell made the native artillery useless. Even so, in the autumn of 1854, I safely made a trip, about a week long, with Dr. Edkins. Of course, he did the speaking and preaching. I was able to help by distributing books.

In the spring of 1855, I took a trip with Rev. J. S. Burdon of the Church Missionary Society. [He later became the Bishop of Hong Kong.] We faced some serious danger.

In the huge mouth of the Yangtze River, about thirty miles north of Shanghai, lies a group of islands. Tsungming and Haimen Islands are the largest and most important. [In the nineteenth century, sedimentary deposits joined Haimen Island to the northern bank of the Yangtze River.] Farther up the river, where the estuary narrows away from the sea, sits the influential city of Tungchow. It is close to Lang-shan, or the Wolf Mountains, which are famous as a resort for religious pilgrims.

We spent some time evangelizing on those islands. Then we continued on to Lang-shan. There we preached and gave books to thousands of the pilgrims attending an idolatrous festival. From there, we went on to Tungchow. The following journal entries tell the story of our painful experiences there.

THURSDAY, APRIL 26, 1855

After breakfast, we committed our lives into our heavenly Father's care and asked for his blessing before going to this great city. It was a dull, wet day. We were sure Satan wouldn't let us attack his kingdom, like we were trying to do, without raising some serious opposition. But we were also completely sure it was God's will for us to preach Christ in this city, and to distribute the word of truth among these people. We regretted that we only had a few books left for such an important place. As it turned out, though, this was God's plan, too.

Our native teachers tried their best to persuade us not to go to the city. Still, we decided that with God's help nothing could stop us. We told them to stay in one of the boats. If we didn't return, they should learn what they could about what happened to us, and hurry back to Shanghai with the information.

We also arranged for the other boat to wait for us, even if we couldn't get back that night. We didn't want to be stuck on the island just because we were late and couldn't get a boat. We put our books into two bags. Then, with a servant who always went with us on trips like this, we set off for the city, about seven miles away.

Walking was out of the question. The roads were too bad. So we used wheelbarrows, the only method of transportation in the area. A wheelbarrow is cheaper than a sedan because it only requires one coolie. But it is definitely not an agreeable way to travel on rough, dirty roads.

We hadn't gone far when the servant asked permission to go back. Reports about the native soldiers completely frightened him. Of course we agreed immediately. We didn't want to take someone else into trouble. We decided to carry the books ourselves. We looked for physical and spiritual strength from God who had promised to supply all our needs.

At this point, a respectable looking man came up. He warned us earnestly not to go on. If we continued, he told us, we would find, to our sorrow, what the Tungchow militia were like.

We thanked him for his kind advice, but we couldn't turn back. Our hearts were determined. We didn't know whether we went towards capture, imprisonment, and death, or if we would be able to distribute our Scriptures and tracts safely. But we were determined, by God's grace, not to leave Tungchow without the gospel one more day. We didn't want its crowds of people to die in ignorance of the Way of life without anyone caring.

After this, my wheelbarrow man wouldn't go any farther. I had to look for another. Fortunately, a new wheelbarrow man wasn't hard to find. The ride in the mud and rain was anything but nice. We couldn't help feeling the danger we were in, though we didn't waver for a second. Every now and then, we encouraged each other with promises from scripture and verses of hymns.

One verse went:

The dangers of the sea, the dangers of the land,
Should not dishearten you: your Lord is near at hand.
But if your courage fails, when tried and badly
    pressed,
His promise is enough to set your soul at rest.

It seemed particularly appropriate, under the circumstances, and it really comforted me.

On our way, we passed through one small town of about a thousand inhabitants. I preached Jesus there in the Mandarin dialect to quite a few people. I've never felt happier talking about God's love and Jesus Christ's atonement. My soul got a rich blessing. Peace and joy filled me and I was able to speak with unusual freedom and ease.

I was really happy afterward when I heard one of

our listeners talking in his own dialect. He was telling the newcomers the truth I'd been talking about. Imagine! A Chinese man, by his own choice, telling his fellow countrymen that God loved them, that they were sinners, but that Jesus died instead of them, and paid the penalty for their guilt. That one moment paid me back for all the trouble so far. If the Holy Spirit changed that man's heart, we had not come for nothing.

Since the people could read, we handed out a few New Testaments and tracts. We couldn't leave them without the gospel. It's a good thing we did. When we reached Tungchow, we realized we only had enough strength to carry what we had left.

Near the end of our trip we approached the city's western suburb. The prayer of the early Christians, when persecution was beginning, came to my mind: "Now, Lord, consider their threats and enable your servants to speak your word with great boldness" (Acts 4:29). We united heartily in this prayer.

Before we entered the suburb, we discussed our plans so we would be acting together. We told our wheelbarrow men where to wait for us, so they wouldn't be involved in any trouble because of us. Then, looking to our heavenly Father, we committed ourselves to him, took our books, and set off into the city.

For some distance we walked along the suburb's main street, which led to the West Gate. No one bothered us and we were amused by the unusual title they used for us. The called us *heh-kwei-tsi* (black devils). We wondered about it at the time. Later we found out that our clothes, not our skin, gave us the name.

As we passed several soldiers, I told Mr. Burdon they were the men we had heard so much about. They seemed willing to receive us quietly enough. But long before we reached the gate, a tall, powerful man let us know they were not all so peaceful. He was ten times fiercer by being a little drunk.

He grabbed Mr. Burdon by the shoulders. My friend tried to shake him off and I turned around to see what was the matter. Instantly a dozen or more brutal men surrounded us. They hurried us on to the city at a fearful pace.

I couldn't change hands to relieve my muscles so my bag began to feel extremely heavy. Soon I was sweating profusely and could scarcely keep up with them. We demanded to be taken before the chief magistrate, but they told us they knew where to take us, and what to do with people like us. They called us the most insulting names.

The man who had grabbed Mr. Burdon, soon left him for me. He became my main tormentor. I wasn't as tall or strong as my friend, so I couldn't resist him as well. He nearly knocked me down over and over. He grabbed me by the hair. He took me by the collar as if to choke me, and held my arms and shoulders, turning them black and blue.

If this treatment had continued any longer, I would have fainted. I was almost completely exhausted. It refreshed me to remember a verse my dear mother had quoted in one of her last letters:

64

We talk about the realms of the blessed,
That country so bright and so beautiful,
And its glories are discussed so often;
But it must be something to be there!

Oh to be absent from the body and present with the Lord! To be free from sin! And to think that the verse described what would happen at the end of the worst this man's malice could bring on us.

As we walked along, Mr. Burdon tried to give away a few of the books he carried. He wasn't sure we would have another opportunity. The soldier's frightening rage convinced us that in our present situation we shouldn't try book distribution. The man insisted on manacles being brought. Fortunately, none were available.

We could do nothing but quietly submit and go along with our captors.

Once or twice, a quarrel arose as to how to deal with us. The milder of our conductors said we should be taken to the magistrate's office. Others wanted to kill us right away, without any appeal to an authority. But God kept our minds at perfect peace.

During one quarrel, we were thrown together. We reminded each other that the apostles rejoiced that they were counted worthy to suffer for the cause of Christ.

I succeeded in getting my hand into my pocket and produced a Chinese card [a large red paper, with my name on it]. After this, they treated me with more respect. I demanded they give it to the city's chief official, and take us to his office. Before this, no matter what we said, we hadn't been unable to persuade them we were foreigners, though we both wore English clothes.

Boy, those streets were long and tiresome! I thought they'd never end. I've seldom felt more thankful than I did when we stopped. We were told a mandarin lived there. Exhausted and covered in sweat, my tongue sticking to the roof of my mouth, I leaned against the wall. Mr. Burdon was pretty much in the same state.

I asked them to bring us chairs, but they told us to wait. When I begged them to give us some tea. I got the same answer.

A huge crowd had gathered around the doorway. Mr. Burden collected his remaining strength and preached Christ to them. Our cards and books had been taken in to the mandarin, but he turned out to be only a low-ranking one. After keeping us waiting for a while, he referred us to his superiors.

When we heard this, and discovered they planned to turn us out into the crowded streets again, we positively refused to move a single step. We insisted they bring chairs.

After a delay, the chairs came. We sat down, and were carried off, so glad for the rest the chairs gave us on the way. And so thankful we'd been able to preach Jesus in spite of Satan's malice. Our joy showed on our faces. As we passed along, we heard some say we didn't look like bad men. Others seemed to pity us.

When we arrived at the magistrate's office, I wondered where they were taking us. We passed through huge gates that looked like the city's gates. But we were obviously still inside the city. A second set of gates suggested we were being carried into a prison. But when we came to a large tablet inscribed, *"Ming chi fu mu"* (the father and mother of the people), we felt we'd been brought to the right place. This was the title assumed by the mandarins.

Our cards were sent in again. After a short delay, we were taken into the presence of Ch'en Ta Lao-ie (the Great Venerable Father Ch'en). It turned out that he had once been the Tao-tai of Shanghai, so he knew the importance of treating foreigners politely.

As we came before him, some of the people fell on their knees and bowed to the ground. My conductor motioned for me to do the same, but I wouldn't do it.

This mandarin seemed to be the highest authority in Tungchow, and wore an opaque blue button on his cap. He came out to meet us, and treated us with every token of respect. He took us into an inner apartment, a more private room, but a big group of writers, runners and other semi-officials followed.

I told him the purpose of our visit, and begged for permission to give him copies of our books and tracts. He thanked me. I handed him a copy of the New Testament with part of the Old (from Genesis to Ruth), and some tracts. As I did, I tried to explain a little about them and to give him a short summary of our teachings.

He listened attentively. So did the others. Then he ordered refreshments. They were very welcome, and he had some with us.

After a long stay, we asked permission to see some of the city, and to distribute the books we'd brought, before returning.

He kindly agreed to this.

We mentioned that we'd been treated very disrespectfully when we came in. It didn't matter very much to us. We knew the soldiers knew no better. But we didn't want to repeat the experience. We asked him to give orders that we were not to be bothered any more.

He promised to do this also. With every possible token of respect, he walked us to the door of his official residence, sending several runners ahead to see that we were respectfully treated.

We distributed our books quickly and left the city in state. It was funny to see the way the runners used their pigtails. When the crowd blocked the street, they turned them into whips, and beat the people's shoulders with them, right and left!

We had a little trouble finding our wheelbarrows. Eventually, we succeeded, paid off our chair coolies, climbed into our humble vehicles, and returned to the river. At least half the way, an attendant from the magistrate's office accompanied us.

We got back to the boats safely by early evening, sincerely thankful to our heavenly Father for his gracious protection and help.

CHAPTER ELEVEN

WITH THE REV. WILLIAM BURNS

AFTER THE IMPERIALISTS RETOOK Shanghai in February, 1855, I was able to rent a house inside the native city walls. Crowds of people still lived among the ruins left after the war. I was glad to live with them. I made my headquarters here, though I was often away traveling.

This was when God led me to start wearing native clothes instead of foreign ones. Dr. Medhurst, a veteran leader of the London Mission, suggested it. It would make it easier to live and travel inland. The Chinese had allowed a foreign business to build a silk factory quite far inland—provided the building style was completely Chinese. There could be nothing on the outside that suggested it was foreign.

The result of this costume change was very helpful. I have continued to use native clothes and so have most of those associated with me.

By now, the Taipeng rebellion, which had started in 1851, had come to the height of its short-lived success. The great city of Nanking, within two hundred miles of

Shanghai, had fallen in front the invading army. There the rebels had established their headquarters. They went on to fortify their position, getting ready to conquer more.

During the summer of 1855 we made some attempts to visit the movement's leaders. The idea was to bring them some Christian influence. It wasn't very successful, so we gave up trying.

I was one of the missionaries who tried to reach Nanking. It was impossible, so I changed my focus to evangelistic work on Tsungming island. After a while, I was able to overcome the people's prejudice and fear enough to rent a little house and settle down among them. This really encouraged me and gave me joy. But only a few weeks passed before the local authorities complained to the British Consul. I had to leave, even though only three or four miles away the French Consul had been able to get a property for the Roman Catholic missionaries.

I was really disappointed by this unexpected problem. Reluctantly, I returned to Shanghai. I little dreamed what blessing God had for me there!

A few months before, Rev. William Burns of the English Presbyterian Mission had arrived in Shanghai. He was returning from home on his way to the southern province of Fukien, where he'd worked before. Before continuing, he tried to visit the Taipeng rebels at Nanking, like I had. He didn't succeed. Since he'd failed, he stayed in Shanghai a while, spending his time evangelizing the surrounding populated areas. That fall, God led me into a partnership with this dear and honored servant of God.

We traveled together, evangelizing cities and towns in southern Kiangsu and north Chekiang. We lived in our boats and followed the canals and rivers that spread like a network over the rich, fertile countryside of the area.

At the time, Mr. Burns wore English clothing. He noticed that although I was younger and less experienced than he was, people listened to me quietly. Rude boys and curious but careless men followed him. I was invited to people's homes. They told him that the crowd following him made them unable to invite him in. After a few weeks of this, he also began to wear native clothes and enjoyed the increased opportunities it gave him.

Those were happy months. They gave me indescribable joy. I really felt privileged. Mr. Burns had a delightful love for the Word. His holy, reverent life and his relationship with God made his fellowship satisfying to my heart's deep cravings. He told me about revival work and persecution in Canada, Dublin and in southern China. It was interesting and I learned a lot. With real spiritual insight, he often pointed out God's purpose in our trials. His insight gave life a new look and value. He saw evangelism as the church's great work. He also believed we had lost lay evangelism, but that scripture called for it. These ideas planted seeds in my mind. They would bear fruit later when we organized the China Inland Mission.

Our path was not always smooth. Even so, we used every opportunity we were given to stay for a while in towns and cities. We usually left our boats about nine o'clock in the morning after a prayer for blessing. We would carry a light bamboo stool. Picking an appropriate place, one of us would get up on the stool and talk for twenty minutes. The other would be pleading with God for blessing. Then we changed places so the first speaker could rest his voice.

After an hour or two of this, we would move on to another place a little distance away and speak again. Usually, about noon, we returned to our boats for lunch, fellowship and prayer. Then we continued with our outdoor work until dusk. After tea and more rest, we would go with our native helpers to a tea shop. We might spend several hours there in conversation with the people. By the time we left town, it often seemed like the people had grasped a lot of truth. We also put many scriptures and books in the hands of interested people.

Mr. Burns wrote the following letter to his mother in Scotland about this time:

Twenty-five miles from Shanghai
January 26, 1856

Taking advantage of a rainy day that keeps me in my boat, I write a few lines... It is now forty-one days since I left Shanghai this last time. A young English missionary, Mr. Taylor, of the Chinese Evangelization Society, has been my companion during these weeks.

He is in his boat, and I in mine. We have experienced a lot of mercy. In some cases, we've received a lot of help in our work.

I have to retell a story I've had to tell more than once already. Four weeks ago, on December 29, I put on Chinese clothes, which I am wearing now. Mr. Taylor had made this change months before and I discovered that when he preached, etc., he had less trouble from the crowd. So I came to the conclusion that I should follow his example.

At that time, we were more than twice the distance from Shanghai than we are now. We would still be that far away if we hadn't met a band of lawless people. They demanded money and threatened to break our boats if we refused. The boatmen were really alarmed and insisted on returning to some place nearer home. These people had violently broken into Mr. Taylor's boat once before because we didn't give in to their unreasonable demand for books.

We have a big field to work here. It would probably be hard for someone to establish himself in any one place, though the people do listen attentively. But we need God's power to convince and convert. Is there any spirit of prayer for us among God's people in Kilsyth? Or is there any effort to look for this spirit? The need is so great! And the arguments and reasons for prayer are so great in this case. Truly, the harvest here is great, and the laborers are few. And without a lot of grace, they are not well equipped for a work like this. But grace can make the few, feeble instruments into the means to accomplish great things—things greater than we can even imagine.

The incident he mentioned in his letter happened on the northern border of Chekiang. It led to us returning to Shanghai earlier than we'd intended at first.

We had reached a busy market town called Wuchen, or Black Town. We were told the inhabitants were the wildest, most lawless people in that part of the country. We sure found them to be that way! The town was a refuge for salt smugglers and other bad characters. The following excerpts are from my journal, written at the time:

JANUARY 8, 1856

Started our work in Wuchen this morning by passing out a lot of tracts and some Testaments. The people really seemed surprised. We couldn't find any evidence that a foreigner had ever been there before. We preached twice, once in the temple of the war god. Afterwards, we preached in an empty space left by a fire that had completely destroyed a lot of houses.

In the afternoon, we preached again to a large, attentive audience in the same spot. That evening we moved to a tea shop, where we had a good opportunity to speak—until everyone heard we were there. Then too many people came in and we had to leave. But our native assistants, Tsien and Kuei-hua, were able to stay on. Returning to our boats, we spoke to some people who stood on a bridge. We felt we had plenty of reasons to be thankful and encouraged by the results of our first day's work.

January 10

First sent Tsien and Keui-hua to hand out some sheet tracts. After they came back, we went with them. In a space cleared by fire, we separated so we could speak to two audiences. When we returned to the boats for lunch, we found people waiting and wanting books—as usual. We gave some out to those who could read them. Then I asked them to kindly excuse us while we ate lunch. I went into my boat and shut the door.

We hardly had time to pour a cup of tea before a beating sound began. The roof broke in right away. I went out at the back and found four or five men lifting large lumps of frozen earth, dug from a nearby field. I guess the lumps weighed between seven and fourteen pounds each. They were throwing them at the boat.

It didn't help to object. Soon a lot of the boat's upper structure had broken in pieces. Dirt covered everything inside. Finally, Tsien got a passing boat to take him to land a little distance away. With a few tracts, he drew the men's attention away and ended the assault.

We now learned that only two of the troublemakers were natives. The others were salt smugglers. Their reason for attacking us was that we had not satisfied their unreasonable demand for books.

Thankfully, no one got hurt. As soon as quiet settled, we all met in Mr. Burns' boat and spent time thanking God none of us had been hurt. We also prayed for the perpetrators, and that God would use it for our good.

Then we took our lunch and went ashore. Only a few steps from the boats, we spoke to the huge crowd that soon gathered. God gave us extra help. People have never listened more attentively. Not one person expressed sympathy for the men who'd attacked us. That evening at the tea shops, we saw the same spirit. Some seemed filled with joy to hear the good news of salvation through a crucified and risen Savior.

As we came home, we passed a barber's shop that was still open. I went in. While I got my head shaved, I had an opportunity to speak to a few people. Afterwards I pasted a couple of sheet tracts on the wall for future customers.

A respectable shopkeeper named Yao received New Testament portions and a tract on the first or second day of our stay at Wuchen. Yesterday, when our boat was broken, he came to beg for more books. At the time, we were all in confusion because of the damage, and because of all the dirt thrown into the boat. We invited him to come again in a day or two when we would gladly give him the books.

This morning he appeared and handed in the following note:

On a former day I begged Burns and Taylor, the two "Rabbis," to give me good books. It happened at that time those of our town whose hearts were deceived by Satan, not knowing the Son of David, went so far as to dare to "raca" and "moreh" and injure your respected boat. I thank you for promising afterwards to give the books, and beg the following: *Complete New Testament, Discourse of a Good Man When Near His Death, Important Christian Doctrines,* an *Almanac, Principles of Christianity, Way to Make the World Happy*—of each one copy. Sung and Tsien, and all teachers I hope are well. Further compliments are unwritten.

This note is interesting because it shows he'd been attentively reading the New Testament. The words in quotes were all taken from it. His use of "raca" and "moreh" to mean reviling shows he understood what they meant.

After we supplied this man, we went out with Tsien and Kuei-hua to the east of the town. We spoke in the street for a short time. When we returned to the boats, two Chihli men (from the modern province of Hopeh in northeast China) visited me. They're in the magistrate's office here. God helped me considerably as I spoke to them, in the Mandarin dialect, about a crucified Savior. One of them didn't pay much attention, but the other did. His questions proved he was interested.

When they left, I went ashore and spoke to the people who had collected there. Kuei-hua had been preaching to them. The setting sun gave an opportunity to tell a parable. It reminded me of Jesus' words, "Night is coming when no one can work" (John 9:4). As I talked about the uncertain length of this life, and that we don't know when Christ will return, a seriousness, like I'd never seen in China before, settled on the people. When I prayed, the people were quiet and orderly. Then I returned to my boat with a Buddhist priest who'd been in the audience. He admitted that Buddhism was a system without truth that couldn't give hope in death.

JANUARY 12

In the afternoon we talked to the people on shore close to our boats. We also spoke in one of the city streets and in a tea shop. Each time, we gave out books.

In the evening, like always, we went to talk in the tea shops. But we were determined to visit the opposite end of the town so the people living there would be able to meet with us. It was a long, straggling town, nearly two English miles long. Mr. Burns and I usually spoke Chinese together, so those in the boats knew what we decided.

After we'd gone a little way, we changed our minds. Instead, we went to the usual tea shop. We thought people might have gone there expecting to meet us. They hadn't and we didn't find anyone serious about listening like we had before.

Because of this, Mr. Burns suggested we leave earlier than usual. We did so, telling Tsien and Kuei-hua they could stay a little longer. We returned to the boats, giving away a few books on the way. The interesting thing was that we were left alone. No one came with us like they usually did.

When we started, it had been a clear night, but it had

grown intensely dark. On our way, we met the boatman. His manner seemed really strange. Without any explanation, he blew out our lantern's candle. Telling him not to put it out again, we relit the lantern. To our surprise, he deliberately took the candle out and threw it into the canal. Then he walked along a low wall that jutted out to the river's edge and stared into the water.

Not knowing what was the matter with him, I ran forward to stop him. I was afraid he would drown himself. To my relief, he came back quietly. In answer to our repeated questions, he told us not to talk. Some bad men were planning to destroy the boats and the boatmen had moved away to avoid them. Then he led us to where one of the boats lay.

Before long, Tsien and Kuei-hua came and got on board safely. Soon after that, the teacher Sung joined us and the boat moved away.

That was when we learned what was going on. A man claiming to be the constable had come to the boats while we were gone. He had a written demand for ten dollars and some opium. He said more than fifty country people (salt smugglers) were awaiting the reply in a nearby tea shop. If we gave them what they wanted, and three hundred cash [each worth 1/20th of a penny] to pay for their tea, we'd be left in peace. If not, they would come and destroy our boats immediately.

Sung told them we couldn't do what they wanted. We were not traders; we were just preaching and giving out books. We didn't have any opium and our money was nearly all gone.

The man told him plainly he didn't believe him. Sung had no alternative. He had to look for us, so he asked the man to wait for our answer. Not knowing we had changed our plans, he looked for us in the wrong direction. Of course he didn't find us.

Meanwhile, the boatmen managed to move away. They were very worried. They'd just seen what these men did in broad daylight and they didn't want to experience what they might try at night. Moving away, they had separated. That way, if one boat got damaged, we could still use the other one. After that, by God's grace, we met the boatman and he led us safely on board.

As Sung passed the place we'd been moored before, he peered through the trees. He saw a dozen or more men, and heard them asking where the boats had gone. No one knew. Thankfully, they searched in vain.

After a while, the boats joined together, and rowed for a while. It was already late. In that part of the country traveling by night was not a good way to avoid danger from evil men. So the question was, what should we do?

We let the boatmen decide. They had moved off by their own choice, and we felt we couldn't make others stay in danger just because we wanted something different.

We did urge them to do whatever they intended to do quickly. Tomorrow was the Lord's Day, and we didn't want to travel. We also told them that wherever we went, we had to do what we had come to do: preach the gospel. So it didn't really matter where we stayed.

Because even if we passed the night without anyone finding us, they'd be sure to find us the next morning.

The men finally concluded that we might as well go back to the place we'd started from. We agreed to this completely, and they turned back.

Whether by accident or not, we couldn't tell, the boatmen got into another stream. For some time, they didn't know where they were rowing. It was very dark, and at last they moored for the night.

We called the boatmen together, along with our native assistants, and read Psalm 91 to them. You can imagine how appropriate it was to our situation, and how comforting these words from God's Word were:

> He who dwells in the shelter of the Most High
> > will rest in the shadow of the Almighty.
> I will say of the Lord, "He is my refuge and my
> > fortress, my God, in whom I trust."
> Surely he will save you from the fowler's snare
> > and from the deadly pestilence.
> He will cover you with his feathers,
> > and under his wings you will find refuge;
> > his faithfulness will be your shield and rampart.
> You will not fear the terror of night,
> > nor the arrow that flies by day.
> "Because he loves me," says the Lord, "I will rescue
> > him;
> > I will protect him, for he acknowledges my
> > name.
> He will call upon me, and I will answer him;

I will be with him in trouble,
I will deliver him and honor him.
With long life will I satisfy him
and show him my salvation.

God had covered us with thick darkness and allowed us to escape from the hands of the violent. We committed ourselves to his care and keeping in prayer, then retired for the night. Thanks to the kind protection of the Watchman of Israel, who never sleeps or forgets his people, we passed the night in peace and quiet. In some way, he had helped us realize the truth of the verse that says, "You are my refuge and my shield" (Psalm 119:114).

SUNDAY, JANUARY 13

This morning, a violent pain in the knee joint woke me about 4 a.m. I had bruised it the day before. Severe inflammation resulted.

To my surprise, I heard rain pouring down in torrents. The weather had been really nice the day before. Looking out, we found we were near the place we'd stopped before. We were so close that without something to prevent us we would have felt we had to go into town to preach as usual. But the rain fell so heavily all day that no one could leave the boats. So, we enjoyed a delightful day of rest, like we hadn't had in a long time. And the weather prevented many people from coming to ask for us.

If the day had been sunny, we would probably have

been discovered, even if we hadn't left the boats. But we had the peace we needed to think with wonder and thankfulness about the gracious way God had taken care of us, leading us into "the desert" to rest for a while.

MONDAY, JANUARY 14

A cloudless morning. Before the sun came up, one of the native assistants went to get some clothes we'd sent out for washing. He came back with the news that in spite of the drenching rain the day before, men had been looking all over for us. But we had been kept in peace and safety under "the shadow of the Almighty."

The boatmen were so completely scared now that they wouldn't stay any longer. They moved off at dawn. I was confined to my quarters because of lameness and didn't have any choice but to go with them. That afternoon, we reached Pingwang, on the way to Shanghai.

Bad that God blesses is our good,
    And unblessed good is bad;
And everything is right that seems the most wrong
    If it is his sweet will.

CHAPTER TWELVE

CALLED TO SWATOW

WE WERE DISAPPOINTED TO HAVE TO leave the Black Town area so unexpectedly. We'd hoped to spend some time evangelizing in that district. But we would find it wasn't just bad luck. The circumstances that seemed so troublesome were links in the chain of God's plan, guiding us to other, larger places.

God doesn't let persecution arise without good reason. He was leading us by a way we didn't know. But it was still his way.

O Lord, how happy we would be
      If we would cast our cares on you,
If we would rest from self;
      And felt in our hearts that someone above
In perfect wisdom, perfect love,
      Is working for the best!

We reached Shanghai, planning to return inland in a few days with fresh supplies of books and money. In Shanghai we met a Christian captain who had been trading at Swatow. He made a strong case for the needs of that area. British merchants lived on Double Island, and sold opium. They were also involved in the coolie trade, practically a slave traffic. But there was no British missionary to preach the gospel.

The Spirit of God impressed me with a feeling that this was his call, but for days I felt like I couldn't obey it. I'd never had a spiritual father like Mr. Burns. I'd never known such holy, happy fellowship. Surely it couldn't be God's will for us to separate, I told myself.

In great turmoil one evening, I went with Mr. Burns to tea at the house of Rev. R. Lowrie of the American Presbyterian Mission. He lived at Shanghai's South Gate. After tea, Mrs. Lowrie played "The Missionary Call" for us. I'd never heard it before. It really affected me. Before it was finished, my heart was almost broken. I told the Lord, in the words that had been sung:

And I will go!
I can no longer hold back from giving up friends,
    and idol hopes,
And every tie that binds my heart...
From now on it doesn't matter if my earthly lot is
    storm or sunshine, if my cup is bitter or sweet,
I only pray, God, make me holy,
And give my spirit the nerve for the stern hour of
    fighting.

When we left, I asked Mr. Burns to come home with me to the little house I still used as my headquarters in the native city. There, with many tears, I told him how the Lord had been leading me, and how rebellious I'd been, unwilling to leave him for this new area of work. He listened with a strange, surprised look of pleasure, not pain. He said he'd decided to tell me that night that he'd heard the Lord's call to Swatow. His one regret had been the prospect of breaking our happy fellowship.

We went together, and started missionary work in that part of China. In later years, the work there has really been blessed.

Long before this time, Rev. R. Lechler of the Basel Missionary Society had traveled widely in the Swatow area and the regions around it. He was driven from place to place. He did work that wasn't forgotten, even though in the end he had to retire to Hong Kong. This earnest servant of God has kept working for more than forty years. Quite recently he and his devoted wife left Hong Kong to return inland again, to spend the strength of the years they have left among the people he loved so long and well.

Captain Bowers was the Christian friend God used to bring Swatow's needs to our attention. He was overjoyed when he heard our decision to give ourselves to evangelizing that busy, important and crowded market. He was just about to sail back there and gladly offered us free passages on board the *Geelong*. We left Shanghai early in the month of March, 1856.

We had a nice six-day journey. It brought us to Double Island, where we landed in the middle of a small but very ungodly community of foreigners. They were involved in the opium trade and other commercial ventures. Since we didn't want to be identified with these fellow Englishmen, we wanted to get a place in the native city right away. It stood on a piece of land that jutted out from the mainland, five miles farther up, at the mouth of the Han river.

We had a lot of trouble trying to make inroads into this community. In fact, it seemed like we were going to fail completely. We had to depend on the Lord in prayer. God soon took care of it. One day we met a Cantonese merchant. He was a relative of the highest official in town. Mr. Burns started talking to him in Cantonese. The man was so pleased to hear a foreigner speak his language that he became our friend and got us a place to live.

Even so, we only had one little room. I'll never forget the long, hot summer months we spent in that oven! Around the eaves, we could touch the heated roof tiles with our hands. But it was impossible to get anything better.

We made our stay more interesting by visiting the surrounding countryside. The difficulties and dangers we experienced there were so bad—and constant—that it made the work we'd done in the North seem tame by comparison! The hatred and contempt of the Cantonese were very painful. The most common names they called us were "foreign devil," "foreign dog," or "foreign pig." But all of this just led us into deeper fellowship with the One who was "despised and rejected by men" (Isaiah 53:3). It was fellowship deeper than I'd ever known before.

When we visited the country, we risked being kidnapped at any time. The people usually announced that the whole area was "without emperor, without ruler, and without law." That was sure true in those days!

One time we visited a small town. We discovered that the inhabitants had captured a wealthy man of another clan. They demanded a large ransom for his release. When he refused to pay it, they smashed his ankle bones one by one with a club. They got their promise of payment.

Nothing but God's protection prevented us from being treated the same way. The towns were all walled. One town might contain ten or twenty thousand people of the same clan and surname, frequently at war with the people in the next town. A kind reception in one place might mean danger in the next. In circumstances like this, we often saw God's protection.

After a while, the local mandarin got sick. The native doctors couldn't help him. He'd heard from some of my former patients about how they'd been helped. God blessed the medicines I gave him. Thankful for the relief he felt, he suggested we rent a house for a hospital and dispensary. With his permission, we were able to get the whole place where we'd been renting a room.

I'd left my supply of medicine and surgical instruments with my friend, Mr. Wylie, in Shanghai, so I went back to get them. Mr. Burns came down from a town called Ampow. We'd visited it together several times.

He saw me off. Then, after I sailed, he went back with two native evangelists who had been sent from Hong Kong by Rev. J. Johnson of the American Baptist Missionary Union.

The people were willing to listen to them preach. They also accepted their books as gifts, but they wouldn't buy them. One night, robbers broke in and took off with everything they had—except their literature, which they considered worthless. Next morning, very early, some people came knocking at the door. They wanted to buy books. The sales continued. By breakfast time, they had enough cash to buy food and also to pay for one of the men to go to Double Island, below Swatow. He took a letter to Mr. Burns' agent to get money.

People kept coming all through that day and the next to buy. Our friends had all they needed. But on the third day, they weren't able to sell one book. When their money from book sales ran out, the messenger returned with supplies.

I left for Shanghai in early July, after about four months in Swatow. I intended to return in a few weeks, with my medical apparatus, to continue working with Rev. William Burns. A new, promising field seemed to be opening in front of us, and we looked forward to it with hopeful anticipation.

Actually, significant blessing would come to Swatow and its neighborhood. But it wasn't God's purpose for either of us to stay and reap the harvest. Soon after I left, Mr. Burns was arrested in the interior and imprisoned by the Chinese authorities. He was sent to Canton. Though he returned to Swatow after the war [the second war between Great Britain and China, beginning in 1856], he was called away to do something else. That kept him from returning later.

My trip to Shanghai turned out to be the first step in a different road, leading to other areas.

CHAPTER THIRTEEN

MAN PROPOSES, GOD DISPOSES

A NUMBER OF DIFFERENT EVENTS came together, in God's sovereignty, to keep me from returning to Swatow. Ultimately they led to me settling in Ningpo, which became my base.

When I reached Shanghai, I was horrified to find that the place where my medicines and instruments had been stored had burned down. All the medicine and many of the instruments were completely destroyed. It seemed like a huge disaster to me. I'm afraid I was like faithless Jacob, inclined to say, "Everything is against me" (Gen. 42:36) instead of recognizing that "all things work together for good" (Rom. 8:28 KJV). I hadn't learned to think of God as the one big circumstance, in whom "we live and move and have our being" (Acts 17:28). Or to think of smaller, external circumstances as being the kindest, wisest and best because he allowed them or set them in place. So I was really disappointed and really struggled.

Medicine was expensive in Shanghai, and I had limited money, so I set out on an inland journey to Ningpo.

I hoped to get a supply from Dr. William Parker, a member of my mission society. I took the few things I had left with me—basically, my watch, a few surgical instruments, a concertina and books for studying Chinese. In those days, Chinese language books were very expensive. I left some of my money in Shanghai.

The country I passed through was suffering from drought. It was the hottest part of summer and the water in the Grand Canal was extremely low. It had been drawn off to water neighboring rice fields and a lot of the water had evaporated in the intense heat. I had decided to make it as much of a mission trip as possible, so I started out well supplied with Christian tracts and books. After fourteen days traveling slowly through the well-populated country, preaching and distributing literature, we reached a huge town called Shihmenwan. Finding my literature used up, I decided not to spend a lot of time on the rest of the journey. Instead I would try to reach Ningpo as quickly as possible, traveling via Haining city.

AUGUST 4, 1856

There was no water after Shihmenwan, so I paid off my boat and hired coolies to carry my things to Changwan. Before sunrise we were on the way. I walked alone, leaving my servant to follow with the men, who stopped frequently to rest.

When I reached the city we had to pass through, I stopped to wait for the others in a tea shop just outside the North Gate. The coolies came on very slowly, and seemed tired when they arrived. I soon learned they were both opium smokers. That was why they seemed tired after only carrying a load one strong man could easily take three times as far.

After rice and tea and an hour's rest (and I'm sure, a smoke of opium) they felt a little refreshed. I suggested moving on so we could get to Changwan before the sun got too hot. But my servant had a friend in the city. He wanted the spend the day there and go the next morning. I objected. I wanted to reach Haining that night, if possible.... So we set off, entered the North Gate, and passed through about a third of the city. When the coolies stopped to rest, they said they couldn't carry the burden on to Changwan. Finally, they agreed to take it to the South Gate. There I would pay them for the distance they'd carried it. The servant then got other coolies.

Like before, I walked on ahead. It was only about four miles, so I soon reached Changwan where I waited for the others. Meanwhile, I hired coolies for the rest of the trip to Haining. After waiting a long time, I began to wonder why it was taking so long. Finally, it got too late to finish the journey to Haining that night.

I was somewhat annoyed. If my feet hadn't been blistered, and the afternoon very hot, I would have gone back to meet them and urge them on. I figured my servant must have gone to his friend's and wouldn't appear until evening.

Evening came. No sign of anyone.

Feeling uneasy, I began to ask around to see if anyone had seen them. At last a man responded. "Are you a guest from Shihmenwan?" he asked.

"Yes," I answered.

"Are you going to Haining?"

"That is my destination."

"Then your things have gone on before you. I was sitting in a tea shop when a coolie came in. He took a cup of tea and set off for Haining in a hurry. He said that the bamboo box and bed he carried, like the one you describe, were from Shihmenwan. He had to take them to Haining tonight. There he would be paid at the rate of ten cash per pound."

From his description, I concluded that my things had gone ahead of me. But by then I couldn't follow them. I was too tired to walk and it was already dark anyway.

Under the circumstances, all I could do was look for a place to stay the night. What a difficult job! After lifting my heart to God to ask for his help, I walked through town to the far end. I thought the news that a foreigner was in town might not have spread that far yet. There I looked for an inn. I soon came to one and went in, hoping to pass without question since it was already dark. When I asked what they had to eat, they told me that cold rice, which turned out to be burned, and snakes fried in lamp oil were all that was available.

I didn't want any questions about my nationality to come up, so I felt I had to order some. I tried to eat it, but couldn't.

While I was doing this, I said to the landlord, "I

suppose I can spend the night here?"

He answered that I could, but bringing out his book, he added, "In these unsettled times, we are required by the authorities to keep a record of our lodgers. May I ask your respected family name?"

"My unworthy family name is Tai," I answered.

"And your honorable second name?"

"My humble name is Ia-Koh (James)."

"What an unusual name! I never heard it before. How do you write it?"

I told him, and added, "It is a common name in the district from which I come."

"And may I ask where you come from and where you are going?"

"I am traveling from Shanghai to Ningpo, by way of Hangchow."

"What may be your honorable profession?"

"I heal the sick."

"Oh! you are a physician," the landlord remarked. To my intense relief, he closed the book.

His wife, however, took up the conversation. "You're a physician, are you?" she said. "I'm glad of that. I have a daughter afflicted with leprosy. If you will cure her, you will have your supper and bed for nothing."

I was curious enough to ask what my supper and bed would cost if I paid for them. To my amusement I found they were worth less than one and a half pence in our money!

Since I couldn't help the girl, I said I would not be

able to prescribe anything for her. Leprosy was a difficult disease, I said, and I had no medicines with me.

The mother, however, brought a pen and some paper. "You can at least write a prescription," she said. "It won't hurt, even if it doesn't help."

But I said I couldn't do that either, and asked to be taken to my bed.

They escorted me to a miserable room on the ground floor. I passed the night on some boards, raised on two stools. I had no pillow, except my umbrella and shoe, and no mosquito netting. Ten or eleven other lodgers slept in the same room, so I couldn't take anything off in case they got stolen. But as midnight came on, I found I wasn't any too warm.

AUGUST 5

As you might imagine, I was hardly rested or refreshed when I got up, and I didn't feel very well. I had to wait a long time before I could get breakfast. Then there was another delay before I could get change for the only [Chinese] dollar I had with me—because it was chipped in a couple places! More than three hundred cash were also taken from this amount (a twenty-five percent loss) because of it. It was a serious loss to me in that difficult position.

I then asked throughout the town for news of my servant and coolies. They might have arrived later, or come in the morning. The town is large, long, and straggling—nearly two miles from one end to the other. So it took a while.

I didn't learn anything. Tired and footsore, I set out for Haining in the full heat of the day.

The trip was about eight miles and took me a long time. Half way there, a village gave me a place to rest and have a cup of tea. I was glad for both. When I was ready to leave again, a heavy rain shower came on. The delay let me share the gospel a little with the people.

The afternoon was almost over before I neared the northern suburb of Haining. I started asking there, but I heard no news about my servant or things. I was told that outside the East Gate, where the sea junks came in, I was more likely to hear about them. I went there and looked for them outside the Little East Gate. No success.

Extremely tired, I sat down in a tea shop to rest. While I was there, several people from one of the mandarin's offices came in. They asked who I was, where I had come from, and so on.

When he heard about my search, one of the men in the tea shop said, "A bamboo box and a bed like you describe were carried past here about half an hour ago. The bearer seemed to be going either toward the Great East Gate or the South Gate. You'd better go to the hongs (business houses) there and ask."

I asked him to come with me and promised to reward him for his trouble. He wouldn't go. Another man offered to go with me, so we set off together. He asked everywhere, inside and outside the two gates. Still no success.

Then I hired a man to make a thorough search. I promised him a liberal reward if he succeeded.

Meanwhile, I had some supper and talked to a large group of people who had gathered.

When the man returned, he had been unsuccessful. "I'm really exhausted," I told him. "Will you help me find a place to stay for the night? Then I'll pay you for all your trouble."

He was willing to befriend me and we set off in search of a place to stay. At the first couple of places, the people wouldn't take me in. When we first went into them, they seemed willing. But the presence of a man who followed us scared them and they refused. I learned that he worked at one of the government offices.

We now went to a third place, no longer followed by the mandarin's messenger. They promised us a place to stay, brought some tea, and I paid the man who had come with me.

Soon after he left, some official people came in. They went away quickly, but the result of their visit was that I was told I couldn't stay there that night. A young man there told them off for their heartless behavior. "Never mind," he said, "come with me. If we can't get a better place for you to stay, you will sleep at our house."

I went with him, but we discovered that the people of his house weren't willing to take me in.

I was so tired and my feet so sore that I could hardly stand. And I had to go looking for a place to stay all over again. I finally found a place, but since a little crowd collected around the door, they asked me to go away to a tea shop to wait until the people had gone home, or they wouldn't be able to accommodate me.

There was nothing I could do. I went, still accompanied by the young man. We waited until past midnight.

When we left for the promised resting place, my conductor couldn't find it. He led me all over, ending up in another part of the city. Finally, between one and two o'clock, he left me to pass the rest of the night as best I could.

I was opposite a temple, but it was closed. I lay down on the stone steps in front of it. Putting my money under my head for a pillow, I would soon have been asleep, in spite of the cold. Then I noticed someone coming stealthily toward me. As he approached, I saw he was one of the beggars so common in China. I had no doubt he meant to rob me of my money. I didn't move, but watched his movements, and looked to my Father not to leave me in this difficult time.

The man came near and stared at me for a while to make sure I was asleep. (It was so dark he couldn't see my eyes fixed on him.) Then he began to feel about me gently.

In the quietest tone, so he would know I was not asleep and had not been sleeping, I said, "What do you want?"

He didn't answer, just went away.

I was very thankful to see him go. When he was out of sight, I put as much of my cash as possible in my pocket. The rest, I put up my sleeve, and made a pillow out of a stone that projected from the wall.

Soon I began to doze. The nearly noiseless footsteps

of two people approaching roused me. Exhaustion had so sensitized my nervous system that the slightest noise startled me. Again, I looked for protection from God, my only support, and lay still, like I had before. One of them came up and began to feel under my head for the cash. I spoke again, and they sat down at my feet. I asked them what they were doing.

They answered that, like me, they were going to pass the night there.

I asked them to take the opposite side, since there was plenty of room. "Leave this side for me."

But they wouldn't move from my feet, so I got up and set my back against the wall.

"You'd better lie down and sleep," they said. "If you don't, you won't be able to walk tomorrow. Don't be afraid, we won't leave you. We'll see no one hurts you."

"Listen to me," I answered. "I don't want your protection. I don't need it. I'm not Chinese. I don't worship your senseless, helpless idols. I worship God. He is my Father; I trust in him. I know perfectly well what you are and what you're planning. I'll keep my eye on you and won't sleep."

At this, one of them went away. He soon returned with a third companion. I felt very uneasy, but looked to God for help. Once or twice, one of them got up to see if I was asleep.

"Don't be mistaken," I said, "I'm not sleeping."

Occasionally, my head dropped. This was a signal for one of them to get up, but I immediately roused myself and said something. As the night passed slowly on, I began to feel extremely tired. To keep myself awake, and to cheer myself up, I sang several hymns, said Bible verses out loud, and prayed in English. It really annoyed my companions. They acted like they would have given anything for me to shut up. After that, they stopped bothering me. Just before dawn they left me and I got a little sleep.

AUGUST 6

The young man who had led me so wrong the night before woke me. He was very rude, and insisted I get up and pay him for his trouble. He even went so far as to try and force me to do what he wanted. This upset me. In an unguarded moment, and with a bad attitude, I grabbed his arm with a grip he didn't expect me to have. I dared him to lay a finger on me again or bother me any more. This completely changed his manner. He let me stay quietly until the guns announced that the city gates were open. Then he begged me to give him money so he could buy opium. Of course I refused. I gave him just enough to pay for the two candles he said he'd burned while he was with me last night. I learned he was connected with one of the mandarin's offices.

As soon as I could, I bought some rice porridge and tea for breakfast. Then I searched for my things again. After several hours of searching without success, I started back. I reached Changwan about noon, after a long, tiresome and painful walk.

Even here, I still couldn't find out anything about my missing things. I had a meal cooked in a tea shop, washed thoroughly, soaked my inflamed feet, then slept until four in the afternoon.

Feeling much better, I started out toward the city, and its South Gate, where I had left my servant and coolies two days before. As I went, God led me to think about his goodness. I remembered that I had not prayed for a place to stay last night. I also felt condemned that I had worried so much about my few things, when all around me were precious souls I hadn't cared about.

I came as a sinner and claimed Jesus' blood, realizing I was accepted in him. I was forgiven, cleaned up and made pure. How great Jesus' love was! More than I had ever realized it before, I knew what it was like to be despised and rejected, and to have nowhere to lay my head. More than ever, I felt how great his love must have been for him to leave his home in glory and suffer like he did for me. In fact, he had even given up his life on the cross!

I thought about him as "despised and rejected by men, a man of sorrows, and familiar with suffering" (Isaiah 53:3). I thought about him at Jacob's well, tired, hungry and thirsty. But he found that doing his Father's will fed him. I compared this with my puny love. I looked to him to forgive the past, and to give me grace and strength to do his will in the future. To follow his footsteps more closely. To be his completely—more than ever. I prayed for myself, for friends in England and for my brothers in the work. Sweet tears of mixed joy and sadness poured down my face.

I almost forgot the road. Before I realized it, I had reached my destination.

Outside the South Gate, I got a cup of tea, asked about my lost luggage and talked about Jesus' love. Then I entered the city. After asking around a lot (in vain), I left it by the North Gate.

I felt refreshed in both mind and body because of that fellowship with God on my walk to the city. I'd be able to finished the last six miles back to Shihmenwan that evening, I thought. But first I went to another tea shop to buy some native cakes. I was eating them when one of the coolies who had carried my things on the first stage came in. He told me that after I left them, they had taken my luggage to the South Gate. There, my servant went away. When he returned, he said I had gone on, and that he wasn't going to start right away. He would spend the day with his friend, then rejoin me. They took the things to his friend's house and left them there.

I got the coolie to go to the house with me. There, I learned the man had spent the day and night with them. The next morning, he had called other coolies and set off for Hangchow. This was all I could find out. Since I couldn't do anything but go on to Shanghai as quickly as possible, I left the city again.

By now it was too late to go to Shihmenwan. I looked to my Father, knowing he could meet all my needs and he gave me another token of his never-ending love and care. I was invited to sleep on a long boat [a passenger boat] which now rested on the river's dry bed. The night was very cold and the mosquitoes bothersome. Even so, I got a little rest. At sunrise I rose and continued my journey.

AUGUST 7

At first I felt really sick. I had a sore throat. But I thought about God's incredible goodness to help me bear the day's heat and the night's cold for so long. I also felt like a huge load had been taken off my mind. I had committed myself and what happened to me to the Lord. If it was for my good and for his glory, I knew I would get my things back. If not, it would be for the best.

The worst part of my trip was almost over, I hoped. This hope helped me continue, though I was tired and my feet were sore. When I reached Shihmenwan, I ate breakfast. I found I still had 810 in cash. The long-boat fare to Kashing would cost 120. From there to Shanghai would be 360. That would leave me just 330—a little over twelve pence—to provide for my needs for three or four days.

I went to the boat office immediately. To my dismay, I found that because the river was so dry, no goods had come down. That meant no boat would be leaving today, possibly none tomorrow.

"Aren't there any letter boats going to Kashing?" I asked.

They had already left. The only other option was to find out if any private boats were going and would let me go along. My search was hopeless. The problem was that no one with a boat wanted to go all the way to Shanghai.

At that moment, I spotted a letter boat heading toward Kashing, just at a turn in the canal. It must be one of the Kashing boats that was unexpectedly held up, I thought. I set off after it as fast as I could, tiredness and sore feet forgotten.

After about a mile's chase, I caught up with it. "Are you going to Kashing?" I called out.

"No," was the only answer.

"Are you going in that direction?"

"No."

"Will you give me a ride as far as you do go that way?"

Still, "No," and nothing more.

Completely discouraged and exhausted, I sank onto the grass and fainted.

Voices reached my ear as consciousness returned. They were talking about me. "He speaks pure Shanghai dialect," one said.

From their speech, I knew they were Shanghai people themselves. Raising myself up, I saw that they were on a large long boat on the other side of the canal. After a few words, they sent their small boat to fetch me and I went on board the junk. They were very kind, and gave me some tea. When I had recovered some and was able to eat, they gave me food.

Taking my shoes and socks off made my feet feel better, and the boatman kindly gave me hot water to wash them. When they heard my story and saw the blisters on my feet, they obviously felt sorry for me. They hailed every boat that passed to see if it was going my way.

I had a few hours' sleep. Since we didn't find a boat to take me, I went ashore with the captain. I intended to preach in the Kwan-ti temple. Before I left the junk, however, I told the captain and the others on board that I couldn't help myself any more. I didn't have the strength to walk to Kashing. And since I hadn't been able to get passage today, I wouldn't have enough money to take me there by letter boat, anyway. Letter boat was an expensive way to travel. I didn't know how the God I served would help me, but I was sure he would. For now, my job was to serve him where I was. I also told them that the help I knew would come should be evidence to them of the truth of the religion I and others in Shanghai preached.

On our way to the town, I was talking with the captain when we saw a letter boat coming. The captain pointed it out. I reminded him I no longer had enough money to pay my way on it. He hailed it anyway. It was going to a place about nine English miles from Shanghai. From there, one of the boatmen would carry the mail overland to the city.

"This man is a foreigner from Shanghai," the captain said. "He has been robbed and doesn't have any way back. If you will take him with you as far as you go, then hire a sedan chair to carry him the rest of the way, he'll pay you in Shanghai. As you can see, my boat is aground over there because the water is low. It can't go anywhere. I will stand surety. If this gentleman doesn't pay you when you get to Shanghai, I'll pay you when you come back."

This unasked-for kindness from a Chinese man, who was a perfect stranger, will seem more unusual to those who know the Chinese. They are usually very reluctant to risk their money.

The people on the letter boat agreed and took me on board as a passenger. How thankful I felt for this intervention by God, and to be on my way to Shanghai again!

Letter boats, like the one I now traveled on, are long and narrow and have limited room inside. You have to lie down the whole time they are moving because the slightest movement can easily upset them. This was no trouble for me. On the contrary, I was happy to be quiet. They are the quickest boats I have seen in China. Each one is worked by two men. They relieve each other continuously night and day. They row with their feet, and paddle with their hands. Or if the wind is favorable, they row with their feet, and manage a small sail with one hand, while steering with the other.

After a pleasant, speedy trip, I reached Shanghai safely on August 9, by the help of him who said, "Never will I leave you; never will I forsake you" (Heb. 13:5) and "Surely I am with you always, to the very end of the age" (Matthew 28:20).

CHAPTER FOURTEEN

PROVIDENTIAL GUIDANCE

BY NOW IT SEEMED OBVIOUS THAT my servant had deliberately stolen the stuff I'd lost, basically everything I owned in China except a little money I'd left in Shanghai. And he had taken it to Hangchow.

The most important question was, what was the best way to handle it so it would bring good to the man who'd caused all the trouble? It would be easy to do something to bring punishment down on him. The chance of him repaying me wasn't very good, though. What weighed on me most was that the thief was a man I'd labored and prayed over for salvation. We'd read the Sermon on the Mount together. To prosecute him wouldn't go along with its teaching about resisting evil.

I finally decided his soul was more valuable than the £40 worth of stuff I'd lost. I wrote and told him this, urging him to repent and put his faith in the Lord Jesus Christ. This decision touched my Christian friends in England. One of them [Mr. George Müller of Bristol] later felt led to send me a check for £40. It was the first of many.

Collecting the little money left in Shanghai, I set out for Ningpo again, to get Dr. Parker's help in replacing the medicines I'd lost by fire. When I'd done this, I returned to Shanghai again, on the way to Swatow. I hoped to rejoin my dear friend Mr. Burns in the work in that important center. God had another plan. The delay caused by the robbery was just enough to keep me from starting south as I'd intended.

Storm clouds had been gathering over the political horizon. They threatened war. Early in October of 1856, the Lorcha "Arrow" incident at Canton led to a definite beginning of hostilities. Soon China was deeply involved in a second prolonged struggle with foreign powers. [The first was the "Opium War" of 1839-42.] At least in the south, missionary work was mostly suspended. News of what was happening, and letters from Mr. Burns arrived just in time to meet me in Shanghai as I was leaving for Swatow. I couldn't help realizing God's hand had closed the door I had really wanted to walk through.

While I was in Ningpo, I had met Mr. John Jones. With Dr. Parker, he represented the Chinese Evangelization Society there. Since I couldn't go to Swatow, I decided to join these brothers in the Ningpo work. I left immediately.

On the afternoon of the second day, already about thirty miles away from Shanghai, Mr. Jones and I were getting close to the large, important city of Sungkiang. I talked about going ashore to preach the gospel to the crowds of people lining the banks and crowding the roads into the city.

Among the passengers on board the boat was one intelligent man who'd been abroad a lot. He had even visited England, where he had gone by the name Peter. As you might expect, he had heard some of the gospel, but he'd never experienced its saving power. The evening before, I had drawn him into a serious conversation about his soul's salvation. He listened attentively, and even started to cry, but we still couldn't see any definite result. So I was pleased when he asked us to let him go along and hear me preach.

I went into the boat's cabin to get tracts and books ready for distribution when we landed. Suddenly, a splash and a cry outside startled me. I leaped on deck and took in everything at a glance. Peter was gone! The other men were all there, looking helplessly at the spot where he'd disappeared. No one tried to save him. A strong wind carried the junk rapidly forward in spite of a steady current in the opposite direction. The low, shrubless shore offered no landmark to show how far we had left the drowning man behind.

Immediately, I let down the sail and jumped overboard in hope of finding him. I was unsuccessful. In agonizing suspense, I looked around. Close to me, I spotted a fishing boat which had a peculiar dragnet with hooks. I knew it would bring him up.

"Come!" I yelled, as hope returned. "Come, drag over this spot immediately! A man is drowning right here!"

"*Veh bin*" (It's not convenient), they answered.

"Don't talk about convenience!" I said in agony. "A man is drowning, I tell you!"

"We're busy fishing," they answered, "and can't come."

"Never mind your fishing," I said. "I'll give you more money than many day's fishing will bring. Just come—come now!"

"How much money will you give us?"

"We can't discuss that now! Come, or it'll be too late. I'll give you five dollars [then about one and a half pounds English money]."

"We won't do it for that," the men replied. "Give us twenty dollars, and we'll drag."

"I don't have that much. Oh, come quickly. I'll give you all I have."

"How much would that be?"

"I don't know exactly. About fourteen dollars."

Finally, but slowly, they paddled the boat over and let the net down. In less than a minute, they brought up the missing man's body. The fishermen clamored indignantly because their exorbitant demand had to wait while I tried to revive the man. It was too late; life was gone.

To me, this incident was profoundly sad and very significant. Weren't those fishermen actually guilty of the poor man's death? They'd had the ability to save him right there, if they would have used it. I know they were guilty.

But before we judge them, we need to stop and think. Someone greater than Nathan might say, "You're the man!" (2 Sam. 12:7). Is it that hardhearted and wicked to neglect saving the body? How much worse punishment will the person get who leaves the soul to perish? Who say, like Cain did, "Am I my brother's keeper?" (Gen. 4:9). The Lord Jesus commands—commands me, commands you—to "go into all the world and preach the good news to all creation" (Mark 16:15).

Will we tell him it's not convenient? Will we tell him we're busy fishing and can't go? That we've just bought five yoke of oxen, or have married, or are busy doing other more interesting things, and can't go? Before long "we will all stand before God's judgment seat" where "each of us will give an account of himself to God" [Rom. 14:10,12]. So, let's remember, let's pray for, let's work for the unevangelized Chinese. Or we will sin against our own souls. Let's consider the one who said, "If you say, 'But we knew nothing about this,' does not he who weighs the heart perceive it? Does not he who guards your life know it? Will he not repay each person according to what he has done?" (Prov. 24:12).

> Through midnight gloom from Macedon,
> The cry of thousands joined as one,
> The speaking silence of despair
> Is eloquent in dreadful prayer:
> The soul's extremely bitter cry,
> "Come here and help us, or we'll die."
>
> How mournfully it echoes on,
> For half the world is Macedon;

These brothers to their brothers call,
And by the Love which loves them all,
And by the whole world's Life they cry,
"O you who live, come see, we die!"

By other sounds the world is won
Than the sound that wails from Macedon;
The roar of gain is louder still,
Or the call to bow to their own will,
They can't quite hear the distant cry,
"O hear and help us, or we'll die!"

But with that cry from Macedon
The moving force of Christ goes on:
"I come; who will endure my day?
And in those places make my way?
My voice is crying in their cry,
Help the dying, or you will die."

For men you came as Man the Son,
And it's you we hear in Macedon;
Oh, by the kingdom and the power
And glory of your coming hour,
Wake hearts and wills to hear their cry;
Help us to help them, or we'll die.

(Samuel J. Stone, 1871)

CHAPTER FIFTEEN

SETTLEMENT IN NINGPO

THE AUTUMN OF 1856 WAS WELL advanced before I reached Ningpo. It was one of the oldest and most influential cities on China's coast. It had been opened to foreigners in 1842 by the treaty of Nanking, and missionaries had been working there a long time. On its crowded streets, the busy tide of life ran high. Four hundred thousand human beings lived in or around the five-mile circuit of its ancient walls. Every one was a soul Jesus loved and died for.

As winter came on, I rented a native house in Wugyiao-deo, or Lake Head Street. It wasn't a terribly comfortable place at the time. I have a very distinct memory of tracing my initials on the snow that had collected on my blanket during the night. I slept in the large barnlike upper room that has now been subdivided into four or five smaller rooms with good ceilings. If they are sound, the roof tiles of a Chinese house with no ceiling can keep the rain off. But it doesn't give good protection against the snow, which beats its way in through the cracks.

But although the little house may have been unfinished, it was appropriate for working among the people. I settled down there thankfully, and found plenty of ways to serve, morning, noon and night.

During the last part of the year, I thought a lot about whether to continue my connection with my mission. It was often in debt. I had always avoided debt myself and kept within my salary, though sometimes only by being extremely frugal. Just now, it wasn't hard to keep within my salary. My income was larger and the country was more peaceful, so things didn't cost so much. But the mission itself was in debt. The quarterly amounts I and others were told to take out were often met by borrowed money.

I began corresponding with the mission about this. Our letters stopped the following year when I resigned, for reasons of conscience.

To me, it seemed that the Word was clear and unmistakable: "Owe no man any thing" (Rom. 13:8 KJV). As I saw it, to borrow money implied a contradiction of scripture. It confessed that God had held back from giving some good thing, and that we were going to get for ourselves what he hadn't given. Could what was wrong for one Christian be right for a group of Christians? Or could any number of precedents justify taking a wrong course? If the Word taught me anything, it taught me to have nothing to do with debt.

I couldn't believe God was poor, that he might run out of money, or that he didn't want to provide for the needs of a work that really belonged to him. It seemed to me that if there wasn't enough money to carry on a particular work, then it couldn't be God's work—at least not to that degree, in that particular way, or at that time. So, to satisfy my conscience, I had to resign from the mission which had paid my salary so far.

It gave me a lot of satisfaction that God led my friend and colleague Mr. Jones the same way. He was also with the Chinese Evangelization Society. We were both extremely thankful that the separation happened without any bad feelings on either side. In fact, we had the joy of knowing that several committee members agreed with the step we took, even though the whole society couldn't agree with us.

We depended only on God to supply us. We were also able to keep connected to former supporters to some extent. We could still send newsletters home to be published like we had before. This lasted as long as the mission continued to exist.

The step we had taken did test our faith. I really wasn't sure what God wanted me to do. Would he continue to meet my needs so I could continue working like I had before? I had no friends I could expect anything from. I didn't know how God would provide, but I was willing to give all my time to evangelizing the lost if he would supply just enough to live on. If he didn't want to do this, I was ready to do whatever work I might need to do, giving all my extra time to more mission-oriented efforts. But God blessed and prospered me.

I felt so glad, so thankful when the separation finally came! I could look right up into my Father's face with a satisfied heart. I was ready, by his grace, to do the next thing he might teach me. I felt very sure of his loving care.

I can't tell you how much blessing I experienced as he lead me on and provided for me. It was like a continuation of some of my earlier experiences at home.

My faith didn't go untried. It failed pretty often. I was so sorry and ashamed of my failure to trust such a good Father. But I was learning to know him! Even at the time, I would never have wanted to miss the trial. He became so near, so real, so intimate. The occasional difficulty about funds never came from not having enough for personal needs. It came as a result of ministering to the needs of so many hungry and dying people around us.

Much harder trials eclipsed these difficulties. They were deeper, and so they produced richer fruits. I am now so glad to know what dear Miss Havergal said, that "They who trust him wholly find him wholly true." And not only that. I am also glad to know that when we fail to trust completely, he is still unchangingly faithful. He is wholly, completely true whether we trust or not. "If we are faithless, he will remain faithful, for he cannot disown himself" (2 Timothy 2:13). But how much we dishonor God when we fail to trust him! And what peace, blessing and triumph we lose by sinning against the faithful One. May we never be so presumptuous that we doubt him again.

The year 1857 was a time of trouble. It closed with the notorious Canton bombing by the British and the beginning of our second Chinese war. Troublesome rumors flew everywhere. In many places, missionaries faced considerable danger. This was especially true in Ningpo. So God's preserving care in answer to prayer was really obvious.

When the terrible news about the bombing of Canton reached the Cantonese in Ningpo, their anger and indignation knew no limits. They immediately got to work, plotting the destruction of all the foreigners living in the city and area. Everyone knew the foreigners met for worship every Sunday evening at one of the missionary houses. The plan was to surround the place and make short work of everyone there, later killing anyone who might not be there at the time.

They easily got the sanction of the Tao-t'ai, or chief civil magistrate of the city. Now they only had to do it. The foreigners were, of course, completely ignorant of the plot. A similar plot was carried out against the Portuguese a few months later. Between fifty and sixty were massacred in open daylight.

It so happened, though, that one of the people who knew about the conspiracy had a friend who served the missionaries. Anxious for his friend's safety, he warned him of the coming danger and urged him to leave his job with the foreigners. The servant told his master, so the little community became aware of their danger. Realizing how grave the situation was, they decided to meet together at one of their houses to seek the Most High's protection, and to hide under the shadow of his wings. They didn't meet in vain.

At the exact time they were praying, the Lord was working. He led a mandarin, the Superintendent of Customs, to call on the Tao-t'ai. He argued with him about the folly of allowing such an attempt. He assured the Tao-t'ai it would rouse the foreigners in other places to come with armed forces to avenge the deaths. They would raze the city to the ground.

The Tao-t'ai replied that when the foreigners came, he would deny knowing anything about the plot. They would direct their vengeance against the Cantonese, who would then be destroyed. "We'll get rid of both the Cantonese and foreigners at the same time."

The Superintendent of Customs assured him it would be useless to avoid trouble. Finally, the Tao-t'ai sent to the Cantonese, withdrawing his permission. He prohibited the attack. This happened at the very time we were asking the Lord to protect us, though we didn't find the facts out until weeks later. So once more God lead us to prove that: "Sufficient is His arm alone, and our defense is sure."

I can't even try to give a historical record of what happened during this time. But before 1857 ended, Mr. Jones and I were encouraged by signs of blessing.

It's interesting to remember the circumstances connected with the encouraging first profession of faith in Christ. I was preaching the good news of salvation through the finished work of Christ when a middle-aged man stood up. He gave a testimony in front of his countrymen who had gathered there. He told them about his faith in the gospel's power. "I have looked for the truth a long time," he said earnestly, "as my fathers did before me. But I never found it. I have traveled far and near, but without getting it. I have found no rest in Confucianism, Buddhism or Taoism. But I do find rest in what I have heard here tonight. From now on, I am a believer in Jesus."

This man was one of the leading officers of a sect of reformed Buddhists in Ningpo. A short time after his confession of faith in the Savior, the sect had a meeting. I went to it with him. He testified to the people he'd worshiped with about the peace he'd received by believing. Soon after that, one of his former companions was converted and baptized. Both are now with Jesus.

The first of these two continued to preach to his countrymen about the good news for a long time. A few nights after his conversion, he asked how long the gospel had been known in England. We had known it for hundreds of years, we told him.

"What!" he said, amazed. "Is it possible that for hundreds of years you have known this good news and only now you come to preach it to us? My father looked for the truth for more than twenty years and died without finding it. Oh, why didn't you come sooner?"

A whole generation has passed away since I heard that sad question. But how many today might repeat the same question? More than two hundred million have been swept into eternity since then—without being offered salvation. How long will this continue? How long will the Master's words, "to every creature," be left unheeded?

CHAPTER SIXTEEN

TIMELY SUPPLIES

GOD OFTEN BRINGS HIS PEOPLE INTO difficulties on purpose, so they'll get to know him in a way they couldn't know him otherwise. Then he reveals himself as a "very present help in trouble." It really gladdens your heart when you see each fresh revelation of a Father's faithfulness. We only get to see such a small part of the sweet side of trials. And if we only see a tiny bit and still often feel we wouldn't have missed the trials for anything, how much more will we bless and magnify his name when every hidden thing comes to light!

In the fall of 1857, just one year after I settled in Ningpo, something happened that really strengthened our faith in God's lovingkindness and always-watchful care.

A brother in the Lord, Rev. John Quarterman of the American Presbyterian Mission North, got smallpox. It was my sad privilege to nurse him through his suffering illness to its fatal end. When it was all over, I had to get rid of the clothes I'd worn while nursing so they wouldn't infect anyone.

I didn't have enough money on me to buy what I needed to make this change. Prayer was my only resource. The Lord answered it by the unexpected arrival of a long-lost box of clothes from Swatow. They had remained with Rev. William Burns when I left him for Shanghai in the early summer of the previous year. The arrival of the things just at that time was good timing, but it was also amazing. It brought me a sweet feeling that the Father himself had provided for me.

About two months later, I wrote the following:

November 18, 1857

Many people seem to think I'm really poor. This is true enough in one way. But I thank God it is "poor, yet making many rich; having nothing, and yet possessing everything" (2 Cor. 6:10). "And my God will meet all your needs" (Phil. 4:19). To him be all glory! I wouldn't be different if I could. I like being totally dependent on the Lord, and used as a channel of help for others.

On Saturday, November 4, our regular home mail arrived. That morning, as usual, we had given breakfast to the destitute, seventy in all. Sometimes there are less than forty. At other times over eighty. They come every day, except on the Lord's Day because we can't manage to take care of them and get through all our other duties, too.

On that Saturday morning, we paid all our expenses and got what we needed for the next day. That didn't leave us a single dollar between us. We didn't know how the Lord would provide for Monday.

Over our mantelpiece hung two scrolls in Chinese characters. One said, "Ebenezer," meaning "thus far the Lord has helped us" (2 Sam. 7:12). The other said, "Jehovah-Jireh," meaning "the Lord will provide" (Gen. 22:14). He kept us from doubting, even for a minute. That day, the mail came in a week sooner than expected, and Mr. Jones received a check for $214! We thanked God and took courage.

The check was taken to a merchant. Though there is usually several days' delay in getting the cash, this time he said, "Send for it on Monday." We sent, and though he hadn't been able to buy all the dollars, he let us have seventy on account. Everything taken care of! Oh, it's sweet to live so directly dependent on the Lord who never fails us.

On Monday, the poor had their breakfast as usual. We hadn't told them not to come. We were sure it was the Lord's work and that he would provide. But we couldn't help letting our eyes fill with grateful tears when we saw that God didn't just meet our needs. The widow, the orphan, the blind and the lame, the friendless and the destitute were provided for together by the bounty of the One who feeds the ravens.

Glorify the Lord with me;
    let us exalt his name together ...
Taste and see that the Lord is good;
    blessed is the man who takes refuge in him.
Fear the Lord you his saints,

for those who fear him lack nothing.
The lions may grow weak and hungry,
   but those who seek the Lord lack no good
   thing.
   (Psalm 34:3)

And if it's not good, why want it?

But even $200 can't last forever. By New Year's Day, supplies were getting low again. Finally, on January 6, 1858, only one single cash remained—one twentieth of a penny—owned jointly by Mr. Jones and myself. It was a difficult situation, but we looked to God again to show his gracious care. We found enough in the house to make a meager breakfast. After that we had no food for the rest of the day. Or money to buy any. We could only go to the One who was able to supply all our needs. "Give us today our daily bread," we prayed.

After prayer, and thinking through the situation, we thought maybe we should sell something we owned to meet our immediate needs. But when we looked around, we didn't see anything we could spare. Besides, we owned hardly anything the Chinese would buy with ready money.

We might have been able to get credit of any amount, if our consciences had allowed us to ask for it. But we felt this was unscriptural, and inconsistent with our position. Actually, we had one thing the Chinese would buy right off—an iron stove. But we hated to get rid of it. Finally, we set out toward the founder's.

After walking some distance, we came to the river.

We had intended to cross it on a floating bridge of boats, but the Lord closed the way. The bridge had been carried away the night before. The only way to cross the river was by ferry, costing two cash each. Since we only had one, it was obvious we were supposed to return home and wait for God's intervention for us.

On reaching home, we found that Mrs. Jones and the children had gone to eat at a friend's house. They had accepted the invitation several days before. The invitation also included Mr. Jones but he refused to go and leave me to fast alone. So we went to work, carefully searching the cupboards. There was nothing to eat, but we found a small packet of cocoa. With a little hot water, it revived us a little. After this, once again we cried out to the Lord and "the Lord heard" and "saved (us) out of all (our) troubles" (Psalm 34:6). While we were still on our knees, a letter arrived from England. It contained a check.

Just in time! And it didn't just meet our immediate and urgent needs for the day. My marriage had been scheduled for only fourteen days later. I had been confident that God, who we belonged to and served, would not embarrass anyone who trusted completely and only in him. God didn't disappoint my confidence.

Though the mountains be shaken
    and the hills be removed,
yet my unfailing love for you will not be shaken
    nor my covenant of peace be removed
    (Isaiah 54:10)

Though our faith was tested often during the years the followed, sometimes severely, God always proved faithful to his promise. He never allowed us to go without any good thing.

THERE MAY NEVER HAVE BEEN A union that proved the truth better, that "he who finds a wife finds what is good and receives favor from the Lord." My dear wife was not only a precious gift to me. God blessed many others through her during the twelve eventful years she was given to those who loved her, and to China.

She had a life connection with missionary work in that great empire. Her father, the loved and devoted Samuel Dyer, was among the earliest representatives of the London Mission in the East. He reached the Straits [Settlements on the southwestern shore of the Malay Peninsula] as early as 1827. For sixteen years he labored among the Chinese in Penang and Singapore. At the same time, he completed a valuable font of Chinese metallic type, the first of it's kind. He died in 1843, never fulfilling his hope of one day settling on Chinese soil.

But his children lived to see the country opened to the gospel. They shared in the great work there that had been so much on his heart. When we married, my dear wife had already been living in Ningpo several years. She lived with her friend, Miss Aldersey, and was well qualified to help with all her varied missionary work.

CHAPTER SEVENTEEN

GOD IS A REFUGE FOR US

I RECEIVED ANOTHER ANSWER TO prayer early in 1859. It was a little different, but just as obviously in response to prayer. My dear wife was sick. Finally, I lost all hope that she would recover. Nothing we tried worked. Dr. Parker, who was taking care of her, had nothing more to suggest. Life quickly ebbed away.

The only hope I had was that God might decide to heal her in answer to believing, submitted prayer.

The afternoon arrived when the missionaries usually held a prayer meeting. I sent in a prayer request and they responded warmly. Just at that time, God suggested to my mind something we hadn't tried yet. I felt like I should hurry and consult Dr. Parker about using it.

It was an anguishing moment. Her hollow temples, sunken eyes, and pinched features showed that death was close. It seemed impossible for life to hold out until I returned.

It was nearly two miles to Dr. Parker's house. Every second seemed like ages. On my way there, I had a major wrestling match with God in prayer. While this was going on, God brought some precious words powerfully to my soul, "Call upon me in the day of trouble; I will deliver you, and you will honor me" (Psalm 50:15). Immediately, I felt able to plead the words in faith. The result was deep, indescribable peace and joy. All consciousness of the distance disappeared.

Dr. Parker cordially approved of my suggestion, but when I arrived home I saw at a glance that the change had happened—without any remedy. The pinched look of her face had been replaced by the calm of peaceful sleep. Not one bad symptom remained to slow her recovery.

Since I had been spared like this—in answer to prayer for my loved one—I really felt for Dr. Parker when his wife was suddenly taken in the autumn of that same year. He had to return to Glasgow with his motherless child immediately. This meant he had to make temporary arrangements for running the mission hospital in Ningpo, which he'd been running single-handedly. Under the circumstances, he asked me to take the work on, at least in the dispensary. After waiting on the Lord for guidance a few days, I felt led not only to take on the dispensary work, but also the hospital work. I relied on the faithfulness of a prayer-hearing God to provide for it.

The funds for maintaining the hospital had been supplied by the income the doctor made from his medical practice among the foreign community. When he left, this income stopped. But hadn't God said that whatever we ask in Jesus' name will be done? Aren't we told to seek God's kingdom first, not the money to advance it—and all these things will be added to us? Surely, promises like these were enough.

Eight days before agreeing to take on this responsibility, I didn't have the remotest idea of ever doing such a thing. My friends at home certainly couldn't have imagined I would have a need like that. But the Lord had seen the need coming. The funds were already on the way.

Sometimes there were over fifty inpatients at the hospital. Besides them, a large number visited the outpatient department every day. Thirty beds were usually allotted to free patients and those taking care of them. About as many were given to opium smokers who paid for their board while being cured of the habit. All the needs of the sick people in the wards were supplied free of charge. So were the supplies for the outpatient work. The daily expenses were quite high. Besides these things, a number of native attendants were needed and had to be supported.

When Dr. Parker handed the hospital over to me, he was able to leave money to meet the salaries and working expenses for the current month. He could leave little more. Since I couldn't guarantee their support, his native staff retired. I mentioned the situation to the members of our little church, and some of them volunteered to help me. Like me, they would depend on the Lord. They continued to wait on God with me, believing that he would somehow provide for his own work.

Day by day the stores diminished. They were almost exhausted when a remarkable letter reached me. It came from a friend in England and contained a check for £50.

The letter stated that the sender had recently lost his father and had inherited his property. Not wanting to increase his personal expenses, he wanted to save the inherited money to further the Lord's work. He enclosed £50, saying that I might know of some special need for it. But he left me free to use it for my own support, or in any way the Lord might lead me. He only asked to know how it had been used, and whether we needed more.

After spending some time with my wife, thanking God, I called my native helpers into our little chapel. I translated the letter to them. I hardly need to say how they rejoiced! We praised God together.

They returned to their work in the hospital with overflowing hearts, and told the patients what a God we had! They asked them if their idols had ever helped them in that way! Both helpers and patients were spiritually blessed through this amazing provision. From that time on, the Lord provided everything we needed for maintaining the hospital. And that was in addition to what my family needed to live on. And he provided for other areas of ministry, too.

Nine months later, I had to give up this job because of failing health. I was able to leave more money with them to support the hospital than had been left when I had taken it on.

But not only did God provide money in answer to prayer. Many lives were spared. People in seemingly hopeless stages of disease were made well. And we succeeded in cases requiring serious and dangerous operations.

In one poor man's case, his legs were amputated under very unfavorable circumstances. But he got better so rapidly that both legs were healed in less than two weeks!

There were more permanent benefits, too. Many became convinced of the truth of Christianity. Quite a few sought the Lord in faith and prayer and experienced the power of the Great Physician to cure the sin-sick soul. During the nine months, sixteen patients from the hospital were baptized. More than thirty others became candidates for admission into Christian churches in the city.

So 1860 began with open doors on all sides. Sadly, time and strength were too limited to use them all to the best advantage. For some time, we felt a need for additional workers. In January, we prayed specifically to the Lord of the harvest to push more laborers out into this special part of the great world field. I expressed it this way on January 16, 1860, in a letter to relatives in England:

Do you know any earnest, devoted young men who want to serve God in China? Who don't want any more than their actual support and would be willing to come out and work here? I sure could use four or five helpers like that! They would probably begin to preach in Chinese after six months. And their support will be supplied in answer to prayer.

No one came to help us then, though. Under the continued physical and mental strain of taking care of the hospital with Dr. Parker gone, in addition to my other missionary work, my health quickly began to fail. It became a serious question whether I would have to return to England for a while.

It was hard to face this. The growing church and work seemed to need us. It was hard to leave those we had learned to love so much in the Lord. Thirty or forty native Christians were a part of the recently organized church. Well-filled meetings and the warm-hearted earnestness of the converts spoke of a promising future. In the end, though, I was completely laid out by repeated attacks of sickness. The only hope of getting better seemed to lie in a trip to England and a short stay in its cooler climate. Although it seemed painful at the time, this need proved to be another opportunity to see the faithfulness and loving care of the One "who works out everything in conformity with the purpose of his will" (Ephesians 1:11).

As before, the Lord was there with help at the right time. He supplied the money for the trip so liberally that we were able to bring a native Christian with us. He would help in translation or other literary work, and would teach the language to any helpers the Lord might raise up to expand the mission. We didn't doubt God would give us fellow laborers. We had felt able to ask for them in earnest and believing prayer for many months.

The day before leaving China, we wrote our friend, Mr. W. T. Berger, whom we'd known in England. He had always strengthened our hands in the Lord while we were in China. We wrote:

> We are bringing with us a young Chinese brother to help in language work. I hope he will also help teach the dialect to those the Lord may send with us.

Throughout the voyage, we cried earnestly to God that he would rule over our stay at home for China's good. We prayed he would use our trip to raise up at least five helpers to work in Chekiang province.

It pleased the Lord to answer these earnest and believing prayers and to crown them with "immeasurably more" than we had asked.

CHAPTER EIGHTEEN

A NEW AGENCY NEEDED

"FOR MY THOUGHTS ARE NOT YOUR THOUGHTS;
neither are your ways my ways," declares
the Lord,
"As the heavens are higher than the earth,
so are my ways higher than your ways
and my thoughts than your thoughts."
(Isaiah 55:8-9)

How true these words are! When the Lord pours on the blessings in the best way possible, how many times do our unbelieving hearts feel like "everything is against me"? How many times do we say it, like Jacob did (Genesis 42:36)? Or we're full of fear, like the disciples were when the Lord walked on the water. He came closer to tame the troubled sea and bring them quickly to the safe place they wanted to find.

Mere common sense should tell us that the Perfect One can't make any mistakes! He's promised to "fulfill his purpose for (us)" (Psalm 138:8). He specifically counts every hair on our heads. He molds our circumstances for us. Surely he knows better than we do how to make our truest goals and desires happen. And how to glorify his own name.

Blind unbelief is bound to make mistakes
And search in vain for meaning in his work;
God himself interprets what he does,
And he will make everything clear.

It seemed like a huge disaster when failing health forced me to give up work for God in China—just when the work was more fruitful than ever! And it was so sad to leave the little group of Christians in Ningpo. They needed so much care and teaching!

I felt even worse when I reached England and the doctors told me I wouldn't be able to go back to China. Not for years, anyway. Little did I realize that the long separation from China was necessary. It was a step toward forming a work God would bless. And he has blessed the China Inland Mission.

While I was on the field, the pressure of the needs all around me was so great I couldn't think about the even greater needs of areas farther inland. Even if I thought about them, I couldn't do anything about it, anyway. But while God kept me in England several years, I was as close to the huge areas of inland China as I was to the small areas I had personally worked in for God. Prayer was often the only way to relieve the burden on my heart.

Since a long absence from China seemed inevitable,

the next question was how I could best serve China in England. This led to several years of working with Rev. F. F. Gough of the CMS on the revision of a version of the New Testament in the Ningpo dialect. We did it for the British and Foreign Bible Society.

When I took on the job, I was rather shortsighted. I only saw how useful the book and its marginal references would be to the native Christians. Since then, I've often seen that without those months of feasting on God's word, I would have been completely unprepared to form a mission like the China Inland Mission is now.

As I studied God's word, I learned that the way to get successful workers was not through elaborate appeals for help. It was to first pray earnestly to God to "send out workers" (Matthew 9:38). Second, to pray for the church's spiritual life to deepen so that men would not be able to stay home. I saw that the apostolic plan was not to raise ways and means, but to go and do the work, trusting in God's word that if you, "seek first his kingdom and his righteousness... all these things will be given to you as well" (Matthew 6:33).

Meanwhile, God was answering prayer for workers for Chekiang. The first, Mr. Meadows, sailed for China with his young wife in January, 1862. This came about through the kind cooperation and help of our friend, Mr. Berger.

The second worker left England in 1864. She had her passage provided by the Foreign Evangelization Society. The third and fourth reached Ningpo on July 24, 1865. A fifth soon followed, reaching Ningpo in

September, 1865. So the prayer for five workers had been completely answered! It encouraged us to look for ever greater things from God.

Months of earnest prayer and a number of aborted efforts resulted in a deep conviction that a special agency was essential for the evangelization of inland China. At the time, it helped me to pray and consult daily with my dear friend and co-worker, Rev. F. F. Gough.

I also had Mr. and Mrs. Berger's invaluable help and advice. I and my dear wife, whose judgment and devotion to God were priceless at the time, spent many days prayerfully talking over everything with them. We saw the danger of interfering with existing missions. But we concluded that, by simply trusting in God, an appropriate agency could be started and supported without harming any existing work.

I also had a growing conviction that God wanted me to seek him for the necessary workers, and to go out with them. But for a long time, unbelief hindered me from taking the first step.

Unbelief is so inconsistent! I never doubted that if I prayed for workers in Jesus' name, they would be given to me. I also didn't doubt that the provision for us to go out would be there, and that doors would be opened in front of us in unreached parts of the Empire. But at the time, I hadn't learned to trust God to keep me and give me grace. No wonder I couldn't trust him to keep others willing to go with me! I feared that when the dangers, difficulties and trials came—which of course they would—inexperienced Christians might break down and get upset with me for having encouraged them to do something they weren't up to doing.

But what could I do? The feeling of being blood-guilty became more and more intense. Because I refused to ask, the laborers didn't come. They didn't go out to China. And every day tens of thousands passed away to Christless graves. Dying China filled my heart and mind so much that I had no rest during the day and little sleep at night. Finally my health broke down.

My dear honored friend, Mr. George Pearse, with the Stock Exchange at the time, invited me to stay with him in Brighton. I went to spend a few days there.

Sunday, June 25, 1865. I couldn't stand the sight of a congregation of a thousand or more Christians rejoicing in their own security while millions perished for lack of knowledge. Instead, I wandered alone on the sands in great spiritual agony. There the Lord conquered my unbelief, and I surrendered myself to God to do what he asked. I told him he had to be responsible for what happened. As his servant, my job was to obey and follow him. His job was to direct, take care of, and guide me and the others who would work with me. Of course, the peace immediately flowed into my burdened heart. There and then, I asked him for twenty-four fellow workers. Two were for each of the eleven inland provinces without missionaries, two for Mongolia.

I wrote the prayer request in the margin of the Bible I had with me and went home. For the first time in months, my heart enjoyed rest. I knew the Lord would bless his own work. And I would share in the blessing. Before then, I had prayed that workers for those eleven provinces would be raised up, sent out and cared for. But I hadn't surrendered myself to be their leader.

About this time, with my dear wife's help, I wrote a little book called *China's Spiritual Needs and Claims.* Every paragraph was written with prayer. With Mr. Berger's help, the books were soon circulating. He revised the manuscript, and paid for 3,000 copies to be printed.

Whenever I had an opportunity, I spoke about the proposed work, especially at the Perth and Mildmay Conferences of 1865. I also continued to pray for co workers. They were soon raised up. After corresponding with them, I invited them to my home, which was just east of London at the time. When the one house got too small, the occupant of the adjoining house moved. I was able to rent it. When we also outgrew it, God provided another place nearby. Soon quite a few men and women were receiving training and involved in evangelism, which tested their ability to win souls, at least to some degree.

CHAPTER NINETEEN

THE FORMING OF THE CIM

IN 1865 THE CHINA INLAND Mission was organized. The workers already on the field were incorporated into it. Mr. W. T. Berger lived at Saint Hill near East Grinstead at the time. I wouldn't have been able to do it without his help. He took on directing the home department while I was in China. Every now and then, our friends at home sent in unsolicited contributions. God met every need.

But now we had to get ready to send out sixteen or seventeen. We estimated that it would cost from £1500 to £2000 to cover what they would need, their travel costs, and initial expenses. I wrote a little pamphlet and called it *Occasional Paper, No. 1*. I intended to use later editions to give donors and friends stories about the work we would do in China. In this first one, I communicated what we thought our needs would be.

I expected God to touch some readers' hearts to contribute. I had decided to never have missionaries ask for money personally, or to take collections or give out collecting books. Missionary boxes seemed okay, so we got a few ready for anyone who wanted them. We've used them ever since.

I sent *Occasional Paper, No. 1,* with a cover design, to the printer on February 6, 1866. That same day, we started a daily prayer meeting to ask for the money we needed. It met from twelve to one o'clock. We didn't ask in vain, as the following figures show:

1864	January-December	£	51.70
1865	January-June	£	221.62
	June-December	£	923.63
1866	January-February 6	£	170.41
	February 6-March 12	£1974.30
	March 12-April 18	£ 529.00

On February 6, 1866, we were really encouraged when we received £170.41 because we didn't ask for it and it came in just over a month. We had asked God, though.

But clearly we needed to ask the Lord to do even greater things for us, or a group of ten to sixteen would not be able to leave in mid-May. So, we offered daily, unified prayer to God for the money we needed for initial expenses and travel for the number God wanted to go out in May.

Because of delays in engraving and printing the *Occasional Paper,* it wasn't ready for the publisher until March 12. On that day, I looked in my mission cash box again. We had specifically asked for £1500 to £2000 in a special prayer meeting. The amount in the cash box was amazing, especially compared to the period just before.

Notice that this happened before we sent the *Occasional Paper* out, so it wasn't a result of it. It was the response of a faithful God to the united prayers of those he had called to serve him for the sake of the gospel of his dear Son.

Compare the next period, also of one month and six days. From March 12 to April 18, the receipts were £529. This shows that when God had taken care of the special need, the special supply ended. There really is a living God, and he hears and answers prayer!

But this gracious answer to prayer made it a little difficult to send out the *Occasional Paper, No. 1*, because it gave a need that had already been met. We took care of this problem by including a colored insert with each copy, stating that the funds for initial expenses and travel had already come in, in answer to prayer. It reminded us of Moses' problem, which is not very common today, when he had to have it proclaimed through the camp to stop bringing in gifts for the Tabernacle. They already had too much. We are convinced that if there were less appeals for money, and more dependence on the Holy Spirit's power and on deepening spiritual life, Moses' experience would be common in every area of Christian work.

We immediately started getting ready to sail to China. About this time, I was asked to give a lecture on China in a village not far from London. I agreed, with the condition that they would not take a collection and that they would announce this fact on the posters. The man who invited me, and who kindly acted as chairman of the event, said he had never been given that condition before! But he accepted it. The posters were put out for May 2 and 3. Using a large map, I presented some information on the size and population of China, and its deep spiritual need. Many were obviously impressed.

At the end of the meeting, the chairman told me the posters stated we would not be taking an offering, as I had asked. But he thought many people there might be unhappy and burdened if they couldn't give something toward the good work they'd heard about. If the idea of taking an offering came completely from him, and was what many in the audience wanted, surely I couldn't object.

But I begged him to carry out the condition we'd agreed on. Among other reasons for not taking an offering, the very reason he gave seemed one of the strongest reasons for not taking it. I didn't want people to feel relieved of the emotions they felt by making a convenient donation right at the time. I wanted each one to go home burdened with China's deep need. I wanted them to ask God what he wanted them to do.

After thinking and praying about it, if they were satisfied that he wanted them to give money, it could go to any mission agency with missionaries in China. Or they could mail it to our London office. But maybe in some cases, God didn't want money. Maybe he wanted personal dedication to his service overseas. Or he wanted them to give up a son or daughter, more precious than silver or gold, to serve him.

"I think a collection tends to leave the impression that the only important thing is money," I added. "In fact, no amount of money can convert a soul. What is needed is for men and women filled with the Holy Spirit to give themselves to the work. There will never be a lack of funds for the support of people like that."

My wish was obviously very strong. The chairman gave in and closed the meeting. At supper, however, he told me that in spite of what I had said, a few people had put small contributions into his hands.

The next morning at breakfast, my kind host came in a little late. He admitted he had not had a very good night. After breakfast, he asked me into his office and gave me the contributions handed to him the night before. "Mr. Taylor, last night I thought you were wrong about a collection," he said. "I'm now convinced you were right. As I thought during the night about that stream of souls in China who are always passing into the darkness, I could only cry out, like you suggested, 'Lord, what do you want me to do?' I think I've received the guidance I asked for. Here it is." He handed me a check for £500.

"If there had been a collection," he added, "I would have given a few pounds. But this check is the result of having spent a lot of the night in prayer."

Obviously, I was surprised and thankful for his gift.

At the breakfast table, I had received a letter from Messrs. Killick, Martin & Co., shipping agents. They said they could offer us all the passenger accommodations of the ship *Lammermuir*. I went directly to the ship. It was just what we needed, so I paid with the check. As I said before, we already had the money we thought we needed. But the coincidence of the simultaneous offer of the ship accommodations and this generous gift—God's "immeasurably more" (Ephesians 3:20)—really encouraged my heart.

On May 26 we sailed for China on the *Lammermuir*. Sixteen out of the twenty passengers were missionaries. Mr. Berger took charge of the home department and the China Inland Mission was fully inaugurated.

EPILOGUE

WHEN THE *LAMMERMUIR* PARTY arrived in China in 1866, they faced the seemingly hopeless job of reaching and evangelizing the country's interior. But they attacked the problem with the weapons of faith and prayer. From their bases at Hangchow and Ningpo, they slowly extended their work southward into the coastal province of Chekiang.

As the new workers gained experience, they moved out into Kiangsu, Anhwei, and Kiangsi. This took about ten years. During that time, they suffered a lot from sickness and death, and the bitter opposition of unruly mobs. These mobs often drove them out of cities where they tried to settle and proclaim the gospel. Beyond these cities, even more of inland China still had no Protestant witnesses for Christ.

It wasn't until 1876 that God completely opened the way into the interior to them, having brought them many reinforcements. Then in two amazing years, the pioneers were able to move southwest to the Burma border, northwest to Mongolia and Central Asia, and deep into Tibetan lands.

When we remember China's huge population and the geographical size of the country, we can see that this was a feat unparalleled in modern missionary history. It was accomplished through persistent prayer and sacrifice, not only by those on the field, but also by their friends and supporters at home.

This initial penetration and exploration of the region where the China Inland Mission was called to preach Christ was followed by a period of consolidation. It lasted from 1878 until 1900. During this time the mission grew until its members included many hundreds of men and women, coming from the British Isles, North America, Australasia, Scandinavia, Germany, Switzerland and other countries. They all united under Hudson Taylor's general direction. They agreed to dispense with minor differences of nationality and denomination in their common loyalty to the Lord Jesus Christ and to the central truths of the gospel revealed in the scriptures. Their main concern was to win souls for Christ and to build them up into a living church, worthy of his name. In this pioneer period of the mission's history, visible results were not very large. The majority of those who turned to Christ were simple country people with little education. Missionaries were unpopular, suspected and despised by the more educated groups of Chinese society. He was usually the leader of the Christian community in the district where he lived. Its life revolved around him and its activities were mostly financed through him.

In 1900 this infant church and growing mission were

called to go through the great ordeal of the Boxer uprising. In three summer months, the CIM alone lost fifty-six missionaries and twenty-three children by martyrdom. Hundreds of Chinese Christians were killed. Many other members of the mission endured extremes of suffering as they tried to reach safe places. Looking back, we see that this major sacrifice of life and health marks a turning point in the story of God's work in inland China. And it ends the strictly pioneer era of the mission.

The Boxer Rebellion was followed by a decade when the missionary became embarrassingly popular. He was often seen as the representative of Western civilization. Huge numbers tried to associate with him out of unworthy motives. But the situation also gave unique opportunities. During this time, every phase of the work expanded.

In these days of encouraging responses to the gospel, Hudson Taylor died at Changsha in the heart of inland China. It was the crowning of a life of Christlike devotion and undaunted witness which had few parallels. Few missionaries have seen their prayers so vividly answered and their heart's desire fulfilled so well.

The work he left was tested further when the Chinese Revolution of 1911 broke up the comparative security of the preceding ten years. It ushered in a long period of civil war. In the midst of desperate conditions of lawlessness, brigands and bloodshed, the work of building the church of Christ and proclaiming the gospel continued with increasing fruitfulness. This was especially true among some of the mountain tribes, who turned to Christianity in large numbers.

The international fellowship of the mission survived the strain of the First World War, but conditions in China deteriorated even further. From 1920 onward, atheism and further revolution began to be pushed more strenuously. In the years 1926-1927, it became necessary for the third time for most missionaries to withdraw to places of safety at the coast. As before, however, it wasn't long until they were back in the interior again. Once more, adversity turned out to further the gospel.

After 1927 the mission more explicitly declared the principle that leadership in Christian churches should be transferred from the foreign missionary to Chinese Christians. Now it is easy to see that without this transition, a strong indigenous church could never have risen up. In time, foreign funds were not used much, except to support foreign workers. Chinese believers to whom God had given spiritual gifts carried out the main initiative in the work and direction of the churches. Missionaries stepped into the background of organized church life. During this time, the CIM called for large reinforcements of men and women to bring the gospel to the many millions of people who still lived far outside the reached areas. Two hundred new workers sailed from homelands during 1929-30. The mission's membership rose to its peak of 1,387 in 1936.

Just when it seemed like an era of greater stability was about to dawn under the nationalist government, the conflict with Japan flared up. Before long, the China Inland Mission was divided. A minority lived in areas occupied by Japanese forces. The remainder lived in so-called "free China."

All of those in Japanese-controlled areas were interned after the attack on Pearl Harbor at the end of 1941. They did not regain freedom until 1945. The mission's workers in the West had to withdraw in front of the advancing Japanese. Reinforcements from home were almost completely cut off. At one time, the active membership of the mission was reduced to about 250.

Even so, these years of seeming frustration were rich in blessing. Bible schools for training Chinese Christian leaders started to multiply during and immediately after the war. A remarkable work of God in the universities brought hundreds of students to faith in Christ. These began to replenish the ranks of Chinese pastors with a new type of leadership. When the whole land was thrown open again in 1945, most of the churches so long isolated had grown and prospered.

But it was only after 1945 that the greatest reaping time of all began. Missionaries kept at home by the war, or released from internment, poured back into China. They wanted to take advantage of a rising tide of spiritual opportunity. The past trouble seemed to have plowed up China's soul, making it into ground well prepared for the message of salvation through Jesus Christ. The things Hudson Taylor and the early workers had worked and prayed for were now given to their successors—on quite a large scale. Big meetings became part of the work in some places. Considerable numbers of people from all levels of society were converted. The possibilities of the immediate future seemed limitless, until the tide of civil war surged forward. In the fall of 1948 China began to pass into the control of the communists.

This momentous revolution ushered in a completely new situation. Authorities who had been tolerant or even favorable to missionaries and Christian work were replaced. In their places were people with views based on atheism, materialism and hostility toward influences from the West. Large meetings became impossible. Persecution grew. Christians were suspected of being rebellious. Foreigners were severely restricted in their movements. New recruits couldn't sail, and the total number of missionaries in China went down rapidly.

But it eventually became plain that the continued presence of the missionaries was causing suspicion and harassment for the Chinese believers. So the momentous decision was made in 1950 that in the best interests of the Chinese church the CIM would withdraw.

The China Inland Mission now faced the question of whether it should continue to exist. Was this to be the end, or was there something new in God's plan? It was either extinction or expansion. Discovering great pockets of need that included totally unreached people groups in the countries surrounding China, the CIM decided God wanted them to move forward in new faith. The CIM began again in East Asia, establishing headquarters in Singapore.

A new name, Overseas Missionary Fellowship (OMF), was adopted in 1964 and the old name (China Inland Mission) was dropped. Asian Christians also began to be accepted into membership during this period. Today, more than 20% of OMF's membership comes from Asia.

In the 40 years after the mission left China, 40 people groups of East Asia were evangelized through the work of OMF. God is still leading OMF International, and they are breaking new ground in the most dramatically changing region of the world.

It is encouraging to see that all the major setbacks and supposed disasters of the past have, in the end, proved to be stepping stones to greater things. For sure, this work that God called his servant to in 1865 has been the way for many Chinese to find salvation. Hundreds of Christian churches have come into existence where before the name of Christ was not known. To God be all the glory!

A life like Hudson Taylor's deserves close examination. We find this in the two-volume biography, still in print, by Dr. and Mrs. Howard Taylor. It is a moving account of both Hudson Taylor and the mission up until his death in 1905.

Hudson Taylor's autobiography is an ideal introduction to the above-mentioned book. We invite you to enjoy the more complete record of these wonderful events, and to share, through prayer, in carrying out the command of the Lord Jesus Christ to preach the gospel to every creature. Distance can't diminish the power of prayer. It isn't limited by age, sickness, or other work. Political changes and restrictions can't alter its effectiveness. The word still stands, "You may ask me for anything in my name, and I will do it" (John 14:14). Only neglect can undermine the power of prayer in the life of any obedient Christian.

The text so dear to Hudson Taylor is written over an arch near the entrance to the OMF international headquarters in Singapore: "Have faith in God." In this spirit we look back, and in this confidence we face the future.

DAVID BENTLEY-TAYLOR
This original epilogue has been updated for this edition.

The Missionary Call

My soul is not resting.
A strange, secret whisper comes to my spirit
Like a dream of night.
It tells me I am on enchanted ground.

The voice of my departed Lord, "Go, teach all nations,"
Comes on the night air and awakes my ear.

Why do I live here?
The vows of God are on me and I may not stop to
play with shadows
Or pick earthly flowers,
Until I've done my work and given an accounting of it.

The voice of my departed Lord, "Go, teach all nations,"
Comes on the night air and awakes my ear.

And I will go.
I can no longer hold back from giving up friends,
and idol hopes,
And every tie that binds my heart to my country.

The voice of my departed Lord, "Go, teach all nations,"
Comes on the night air and awakes my ear.

From now on it doesn't matter if my earthly lot is
storm or sunshine, if my cup is bitter or sweet,
I only pray, God, make me holy,

And give my spirit the nerve for the stern hour of
fighting.

The voice of my departed Lord, "Go, teach all nations,"
Comes on the night air and awakes my ear.

And when someone Satan has struggled for,
As he has for me, has at last
Gained that blessed shore,
Oh how this heart will glow with gratitude and love.

Through ages of eternal years my spirit will never
regret
That toil and suffering that was once mine below.

(Author unknown)